PEACE, LOVE, RESPECT...

This is the new way!

PEACE LOVE RESPECT Book Outline:

(I.) Forward

My Thoughts- Though this world seems to be completely manipulated by " " Elite individuals who's entire field of perception is totally myopic and consumed by self service, I know this world can be better!

My Mission- To author a realistic and visionary manifest that depicts in meticulous detail a way of Life, Government, and Society sustaining Institutions based on and uncompromisingly rooted in the principles of PEACE, LOVE & RESPECT.

My Format- I have previously bound my writings to all of the same standards of literary law and grammatical scrutiny as any other Author desiring to be accepted and published. However, I shall no longer. This and anything I write going forward will be expressed exactly how it comes to me. In that form is exactly how I release it to any and all. Life has truly taught me beautiful and important lessons beyond what I would have thought possible. Yet, not beyond what I would have dreamed. For dreams have no limitations. In order for us to earnestly take on the Mammoth task of changing OUR world, we must break loose of the old chains and limitations. This also applies to those set by " literary law and grammatical scrutiny".

My Perspective- Time only exists under the microscope. To experience life through a timeless lens we must view existence from a macroscopic perspective. Science proves that matter nor energy can ever be destroyed, only altered in state. Human beings are made of matter and energy undeniably. Therefore, human beings are immortal on some level and will always exist in some form. Thus, we are in fact ultimately timeless.

(II.) Chapters

Chapter #1-

"Way of Life"

Chapter#2-

"Religions & Belief Systems"

Chapter#3-

"New Governments for a New World"

Chapter#4-

"Our Society Changes"

Chapter#5-

"Families"

Chapter#6-

"An End to Miseducation"

Chapter#7-

"Environmental Responsibility"

Chapter#8-

"Agriculture"

Chapter#9-

"Healthcare V.S. Holistic Wellness"

Chapter#10-

"A Just World Economy"

Chapter#11-

"New approach to Technology"

Chapter#12-

"Open Minds"

Chapter#13-

"We are One"

Chapter#14-

"Moving Forward"

Book Ends*

Chapter#1

Way of Life- PEACE. What does that mean? More importantly what does that mean to you? To me, I think that it means 0. Not to say nothing, or even 0 as a value at all. I mean 0 as in a starting point or as in a foundation to build from completely flat or square. A completely neutral point of origination/creation.

Perhaps that is why PEACE seems to be a concept that has proven to be unfathomably difficult to obtain on this planet. It has eluded the world's governments throughout history. The commonly known story of man on this planet has been littered with conflict to say the least! For as far back as we can peer, man has found reason to compete with man and nature for satisfaction of our most basic needs. That has provided for an atmosphere of unbalance on either side of any significant effort towards PEACE. In other words, man has allowed minor differences to balloon into major conflicts that thrive off of those exaggerated differences, rather than building upon the common areas of growth and potential that we all share. The result of that is a world that has been built on a foundation of division and opposition. This unstable foundation has catapulted this world into a state of unbalance, dis-ease, and ineffective linear systems that permeate every aspect of our lives! Or is that perspective accurate? Has there been any time period when man has found a sort of harmony with man and nature, while meeting those basic needs?

If so then they most certainly would have had to find a place or starting point of 0. A point where neither side of an equation is unbalanced.

Therefore, there is no unmet need or pull of want in either direction negative or positive of 0. This is to say that a truly stable foundation can be built from that point.

So what characteristics do we have in mind when we ponder a solid foundation? The first that comes to my mind is strength. Ever enduring Strength!

Logically, we can state that the life of a structure is dependent on the strength or solidity of the foundation. The base of any sound structure must be strong. This is also true of the base or basis of our "Way of Life".

If PEACE is to be one of the founding principles of our Basis for our "Way of Life", we must investigate this. We need to delve into what has grown into an age long problem to which the answer has been profoundly elusive. So, why so elusive? What has been

the most obstinate obstacle in our path. What immense obstruction has effectively and continually prevented Man from living in the utopia we all have sought for so long? How about inequality? Is not inequality the enemy of any balanced equation? If one man or woman is unequal to any other woman or man can we achieve true balance? Obviously not! So let's take off the blinders of indoctrination and propaganda and have, for many, our first uncensored look at the "real world"!

To truly get to the root of any problem we must think about that problem in a way that lends itself to discovery. We must think with an open mind and in a pathological manner. A true pathologist diagnoses any problem /illness with the same desired outcome, to find the primary or root cause of the issue at hand. Since the problem we are diagnosing is that which has held back the human race from true PEACE, we are searching for that root. We are searching for that initial instance of inequality that has set this paradigm in motion. The single event or interaction that lead to the onset of our problem. Now, let's be real. How can we possibly search back through the annals of time to uncover the 1st actual case of one human being posing him/herself as unequal or superior to another person? Instead , perhaps it is more realistic to search for such interaction between the earliest recorded groups of humans. To do that, we must examine Man's earliest known civilizations, their cultures, artifacts and other clues detailing their existence. Fortunately for our efforts to uncover these aspects of our past, we are given many tools by our ancestors. Early man has demonstrated an innate need to leave many forms of communication and descriptions of what daily life was like for them. They have also proven to have a multitude of means by which to pass that information forward to future generations. Let's take a good look at not only those generations past, but also the myriad of ways that accomplished the task of describing their world so effectively.

Well, before we find ourselves settling in at the most common historical destinations for studying man's early civilizations namely Ancient Greece, Ancient Rome, and of course Ancient Egypt (Kemet,Kush&Nubia), Whoa!
Shouldn't we look a bit further, since there are others whom have left us a clear window into the past? One such civilization is Sumeria or Sumer. This is the civilization that gave birth to ancient Babylon. Many historians suggest that Babylon has been re-birthed for societal emulation and architecturally, in some more modern representations. Such representations show up in the Roman Empire, the English Empire and that of present day U.S. of America. Why? Why and specifically what has been passed on or emulated by the more modern civilizations? We can obviously look at the furtherance of their accomplishments in Agriculture, Physical Sciences, Education, Government(politics), and the Arts. However, we need to be looking at more personal influences that impact a society like the Institutions of Family and Religion. After all, these factors much more directly shape man's daily life and roles on this planet. Take family life for example. Even the most fearsome, empirical and historically recognized dictators have just about all had a "family life". All of which, one can imagine, have their ultra serious and cold exteriors melted away by the warmth and emotionally vital influence of "family life". Which is to demonstrate, that no matter the position, stature or unbreakable demeanor of some of this world's most memorable and historically important leaders, they're all impacted by Family! There's an old saying, "home is where the heart is". I can just picture Julius Caesar strolling in the door after a long "day at the office" ,as an empirical dictator. I can envision him handing his hat and coat to his loving wife with a kiss, and then bending down to kiss his sweet little

daughter(apple of his eye). You get the point, I'm sure. When the heart strings are plucked, even the most formidable figures throughout history, succumb to the basic human need for LOVE. This gives me hope! We can also look to the institution of Religion to see how incredibly profound it's impact on early man's societal development has been. When examining an ancient society such as Sumer or Sumeria, we rely on those previously mentioned historical clues and figurative "breadcrumbs". There are

countless historical artifacts and descriptive texts that give us some insight into this mysterious culture and the beliefs and rituals that comprise practice of religion. One need only turn to the ritual practices of sacrifice and other "blood" rites to be guided toward one dark yet undeniable truth. Which is that from the onset of even our most ancient civilizations man has demonstrated inequality. Also that savage institution of "chattel" slavery flourished in this early society. In fact many of the sacrifices and "blood rituals", were performed using the bodies of innocent citizens and slaves alike. Yet again, I find myself asking Why? Why such a desperate need to dominate other humans to the extent of subjecting them to such heartless treatment? All done under the cloak of religion and belief.

But, what religion? What beliefs? If the sacrifices were considered to be offerings to the "gods", who were these "gods". Better stated who did the Sumerians believe them to be, and why did they require these very violent and bloody acts? What need would a god of any belief system have for these inhumane cruelties? Why is blood such an important part of these sacrifices and rituals? Is it simply symbolic or is there a deeper, more hidden meaning and or purpose in place?

Let's take a crack at answering some of these perplexing questions. First, what religion? The earliest Sumerians spoke a language called Akkadian. The written form of this Sumerian language is referred to as Cuneiform. Anthropologists have uncovered virtual libraries worth of tablets and other artifacts providing great detail about this ancient civilization displayed in Cuneiform. The Sumerians originally practiced a polytheistic religion.This spiritual basis or religious foundation established anthropomorphic deities representing cosmic and terrestrial forces. Sumerian literature of the third millennium BC identifies four primary deities: An, Enlil, Ninhursag, and Enki. It is in fact, these deities that are later to become the subjects of worship in the major modern religions of the world. These deities were often known by other names or attributes in the more modern religions of the world. Christianity, Islam,

Hinduism,etc...are all imprinted with the influence of this early theological belief system. Proof of this shows up in various religious texts from these religions like the Bible and Quran. I'll leave going further into that body of evidence to other writings by other authors dedicated to that genre of literature. However there is a great deal of insight to be had by taking a closer look at what drives those early beliefs, ritual practices,and sacrifices that were supposedly demanded by the before mentioned deities. What are the main characteristics of these deities? Moreover, what did those ancient Sumerians think that these deities required or demanded of those who worshiped them? There are two apparent characteristics unveiled by An, Enlil, Ninhursag, and Enki. All of them displayed anger and jealousy as character traits. So the Sumerians developed rituals of worship aimed at appeasing those character traits and keeping their "gods" satisfied. After all, would a jealous god not demand loyalty? Wouldn't an angry god exhibit wrath? Wouldn't that spur on the subjects of such gods to do whatever they had to do in order to avoid that wrath? Yes, of course they would. For they would be struck with the"Fear of God". Do not many people, to this day, aspire to be good "God fearing people"? While looking into the motivation behind the "blood rituals" and "life sacrifices", some very interesting things pop up. In fact, there are a some incredibly intriguing theories that have been hypothesized surrounding these needy deities and the rituals and practices that the early ancient Sumerians engaged in to appease them. There are those who suggest that the deities worshiped by the Sumerians were actual entities who exist on another plane of existence or dimension. Dimensions are states of existence or density separated by vibration frequency. This can be understood from a scientific standpoint by taking into account that science has long established that nothing in existence is completely at rest. That is to say that, matter and energy of all forms is constantly in vibration . More specifically it is stated that those deities originate from the 4th dimension. We certainly are fledglings in terms of fully comprehending dimensional science. However, it is suggested by many that the 4th dimension is non-physical. That it is what can be labeled as "etherical" as in the properties of ether. It is suggested that the 4th dimension is a vast plane of reality or state of existence that

holds all ideas and thoughts. This is a concept that also holds some scientific water, as scientists have proven that our thoughts are observable and measurable as energetic pulses or flashes. Therefore, the notion that you think a thought and then it just disappears or becomes nothing, is inaccurate. For once an idea is thought, it actually exists somewhere. Where? The current school of thought described above, suggests that the idea would then exist in the 4th dimension as it is an actual thing that exists whether we expound on the idea or not! These deities are proposed to exist on this non-physical plane. Thus, their needs would logically be non-physical. Makes sense right? We'll revisit that later. The concepts of jealousy & fear would logically prompt non-physical needs. Which may cause some confusion when examining the behavior of the Sumerians when attempting to appease their gods. Since, life sacrifices and blood rituals are indeed physical in nature. Obviously, the Sumerians perceived that something about those curios practices ties to the etheric plane or 4th dimension. One would gather that, there must have been something intangible to be gained from these sacrifices and rituals. That's what the Sumerians believed. However, I'm left to wonder something. Where did they get that perception. Some theorize, based on archeological evidence, that the Sumerians had actually come in contact with other worldly beings. These beings are known as the Annunaki. This supposedly a very advanced(perhaps extraterrestrial) civilization is in many ways depicted, by several early human civilizations, through their artifacts. They are said to have influenced all of these civilizations in some rather profound ways. Some hypothesize that they have actually, at some point, interfered with human evolution. Regardless, for our purposes in this discovery process, are not concerned with that possibility. Rather, we are looking to uncover what was conveyed to the Sumerians to influence their religious and spiritual practices, in such a way. What we can interpret of the available evidence is that the Sumerians were made to believe that something very special and of value to their gods is released during the sacrificing of a life in a manner holding to their rituals. The same must be said about blood or certain types of blood used in the Sumerian blood rituals. This actually seems to be a similar belief held by many modern day quote unquote

"secret society" organizations. An example would be masonic organizations. However, there are many who share this belief system. In fact we see some very undeniable ties between these secret societies. Why is that relevant? Because throughout man's history, these secret societies or organizations have undeniably held a great deal of power and influence. This is what some refer to as the "Hidden Hand". That refers to a behind the scenes group of "elites" or unbelievably wealthy individuals with a reach of influence that crosses economic, religious, educational, and agricultural lines. Their influence even crosses national borders with the immense influence they hold over the international banking system and as the controllers of the "World Economy".

In examining the current state of the world, it is not difficult to see the incredibly vast reach of such influence! Look at the conditions that most of this world's population survive in! A lot of folks would say we are doing just that surviving, not Living! Ask yourself who sets the laws and policies that we are forced to navigate ourselves through? Why do the best interests of so much of the world's population seem to be so unrepresented. It's as though the world's governments are not actually looking out for "our best interests"! Rather, they seem to be on engaged in protecting the interests of the world's financially elite. So, why? Why would those whom we elect and trust to represent us create laws and policies that only go toward subjugating and depressing the world's population. Why does it seem that they are in place strictly to uphold the selfish way of life of these elite individuals? Why are the elites so interested in and enamored with creating conditions and circumstances that perpetuate pain, sadness, and misery of the rest of the people, in the world? Well that causes me to more closely examine motive. When I was in sales, I learned about something we referred to as WIIFMs. That is an acronym for " What's In It For Me?". It points directly to human nature and motive. I'm wondering what's the WIIFM aspect of the ritualistic Sumerians and their needy gods? That reverts me back to the question of what the Sumerians and their gods got out of blood rituals and life sacrifices. To answer that, it seems wise to attempt to better understand more about the role and purpose of the blood in blood

rituals and life in life sacrifices. Let's start with blood. Was just any blood used in these sacrifices? No, it was generally the blood of fairly young people of color. Why? Because of the presence of an incredibly complex molecule, MELANIN! NOW, I can go on & on with interesting facts about melanin. For example, most people don't realize melanin isn't just a skin pigment. It's not some cute result of tanning! Melanin has been found in every cell in the human body! Most folks have no idea that melanin is classified as a super-conductor of light, sound waves, electrical energy, magnetic energy, vibration, and even consciousness! For more in-depth study of this incredible molecule, many speakers and authors on the subject can be found on-line. An example would be Dr. Llaila Africa. For our purposes, we can focus on the fact that melanin is found in high concentration in blood. Who's blood? The blood of peoples of color. They naturally have not only a substantially high melanin cellular count, but also the highest grade of melanin (neural melanin). This is why their blood is so vital to such rituals. Also, the reason why younger subjects were preferable is the lack of corruption and years of toxins consumed into the body. Sadly there are also indications that pedophilia was a major part of this as well! Now, as for the demand for life sacrifices and what often proceeded these sacrifices. That would be the ugly practice of torture! Sadly, often times before these cruel sacrifices, there would be very barbaric and savage torture sessions!

Why? This deals with glandular function. Specifically the Pineal gland and the Adrenal gland were the focus of these torture sessions. The adrenal gland, of the two glands, is the most directly impacted by torture. Generally, the idea is to hyper-excite the adrenal gland to cause it to release incredibly high amounts of adrenaline into the subject's muscles, the bloodstream, and receptor areas of the brain. Which brings me to the Pineal gland, located in the brain. The Pineal gland is responsible for the regulation of the body's sleep wake system. It is in control of the production of melatonin and serotonin which regulates mood and many other aspects of human behavior. The Pineal gland is key in the healthy function of the Pituitary gland. It also and perhaps

most importantly is the place in the body where Melanin is actually produced. This is why the Pineal gland was almost always accessed in these life sacrifices. The body fluid containing Melanin would be syphoned out through the connection point at the top of the spinal column and the base of the skull. This was the typical means of extracting the melanin of a sacrificial victim. Alarmingly, this practice is still embraced today by many folks who loyally carryout these same blood rituals and life sacrifices in modern day occultist circles and secret societies. These groups are often comprised of the wealthiest and most famous people in the world, as those are the folks belonging high level Masonic organizations and socially elite! Many of us have heard of world leaders and the most secretive groups of individuals performing Satanic blood rituals and even life sacrifices! That pill proves hard to swallow for the average person who simply cannot believe that such things happen, in this modern day world. After all, isn't this supposed to be a civilized world we live in? Well, we've really stated a lot so far! Within just a few paragraphs, I've introduced some facts, concepts, and unveiled secrets that will likely challenge the entire world view of the average person reading this. Why? Why is this information so shocking? Honestly, there's nothing about me that gives me any more ability to uncover this stuff, than any other person. I don't have any top secret clearance, or secret government inside source! This information is just sitting there available for anyone to learn! So, why are so many people completely in the dark about such profound information! I mean really, this is information affecting us all! Yet, it's known by so FEW, even though this information is openly available to all who do the slightest amount of "free-thinking" research! It feels like a truly ridiculous thing, that the majority of people walk around today, completely in the dark when the light is right at their fingertips! However, it has dawned on me that awakening to this light is an individual choice only. The individual must make an effort to educate themselves in an uncensored, uncontrolled, unedited, and "free-thinking" manner. To do that, unprompted, requires that a person truly have a desire for truth. A strong desire for truth is needed for a person to persist through the obstacles that seem to pop up only after one has truly made progress on this path! It is only with such thirst for truth that

truth can be found. Once a person starts on that path, uncovering the truth becomes easier than you might think! So, then It prompts me to ask, is anyone interested in real PEACE? Whoa! Let's "pump the breaks" a little bit. We'll revisit PEACE or the lack thereof in this world. Plus, to be fair most folks are really just strugglin' to get by. I mean, isn't the average person almost completely consumed by the daily "rat race"? We are nearly all in such a hard core money chase that the average are so "caught up" with it that even "family time" usually takes a back seat! Taking an objective view of all of this, causes one to believe that things are exactly how the elite want them! Furthermore, these elites are just about doing everything in their power to keep things that way! Perhaps, they don't want you to ask questions. For those questions, could lead to an unsatisfied populous. That could lead to those who are unsatisfied to ask even more tough questions of those who have subjugated them. That may lead to more of an understanding of the things that are important to those who run this corrupt world. Subsequently, more questions would come up about the elites, their motives, methods, and how they stay in power! Then, perhaps that would lead to Change! For those who are on top, change is the worst thing to even consider! Even if it means a world with no PEACE!

It looks like it's time to turn our focus towards yet another concept that seems to be absent from our world. That concept is LOVE. I know someone out there is saying" wait a minute love is just an emotion". You're right! Sure it is. However, I am expanding thought on the topic, in considering Love as a concept. More specifically, I'm referring to the concept of unconditional Love. Love as an emotion is something that is familiar to nearly all of us. However, unconditional Love as a concept is something foreign to many. Unfortunately, in today's society love is the 4-letter word that has become the "bad" word. I'll ask you to really and honestly take a good look at how we seem to feel about just saying the word love with, sincerity and depth of meaning. This society generally appears to be uncomfortable with the word. Let alone the phrase, " I love you"! These days love gets lumped into the same category as the "happy ending", the

"good reason" for doing something and of course the no longer popular "good guy"! Nowadays, it's all for "suckers". No one wants to be the "goodie 2 shoes" . Children don't really look up to the hero nearly as much now. Divorce has become just as common as marriage. Movies seem to be ending in sad, depressing or down right negative or bad endings. That's if there even is an ending at all! Often were left to imagine an ending, after the movie leaves us with only that familiar impending sense of doom.

Think about that for a second! Hollywood has decided to start leaving its' audiences with "cliffhanger" endings, only to have us use our imaginations to fill in the blanks of what they've built up as a doom filled climax! Often we're left to see that the bad guy or evil character has won! Now it is certainly realistic that the way a story ends will vary between "good" and "bad". Yet, Hollywood is known for handling these things in trends. Lately the trend has been " No Love" or at least no happy ending! Even when we do summon the "intestinal fortitude" to utter the words "I love you", these days there's always strings attached! The person who says "I love you" to a person always seems to want something from that person, in exchange for love. There's always a condition. Think about it. In every area or walk of life there are conditions being placed on the giving and receiving of love. No one's love seems to come without an exception or condition. A husband doesn't love his wife if she doesn't cook and clean, or vice versa. A wife doesn't love her husband if he doesn't provide for her, or vice versa. A child doesn't show love and gratitude toward the parents without the parent buying them the clothes or video games they want. A friend doesn't love a friend if the friend doesn't do what the other friend wants them to do. You get the point! We live in a society and a world where unconditional love is an imaginary phrase or a concept long forgotten! We as a civilization on a whole have forgotten , if we've ever known at all, what true unconditional love is. We have learned to accept an entire structure of life and supposed civilization where we only know conditional love. It shows up in every aspect of our modern lives. We wake in the morning to greet a family that we love. Yet, would

our love be the same if those family members didn't do the things that we've come to love about them, or rather expect. Further, how is their love for us affected, if we don't do what they have come to rely on us to do. We've all heard the phrase " happy wife happy life"! The only problem with that is that the modern day wife or husband is full of conditions and expectations on love! People have developed a habit of creating and unconsciously demanding certain conditions as requisites for our love. That actually isn't love at all! It's terms for co-dependency! Let's take a look at that. How many of us describe our love or even qualify our love for a person by stating how much we can't live without that person? I mean, we even take that perspective when dealing with the "death" of our dear ones. We find ourselves often emotionally hurt and down right depressed at the thought of living on without that person or persons we hold dear. Many of us can't go through our daily functions of life without placing a phone call to "check-in" on our loved ones. In other words, we depend on almost constant contact and reassurance that these folks will still be in our lives! If that's not dependency what is? In, fact that is paralyzing and perhaps a bit sick! I know of this 1st hand. I have been blessed enough to have raised a family. I have a 26 year old son. I have a 22 year old daughter, and a 20 year old son. I love them all beyond words! However, I have recently begun to examine that undying love. I can honestly tell you that through that beautiful experience, somehow I've grown to have this dependency! How much am I minimizing my love for them, if I'm constantly fearful of losing them. Rather than allowing my mind to frequently ponder such devastating loss, wouldn't I be so better served by using that time and energy finding more and better ways of expressing my incredible love for those, whom I hold dear? How have I arrived at a place where, I demand constant contact and reassurance as a condition for my love? This is not where I want to be . My love is much, much better than that! My love can be unconditional! So, what does that look like? I, along with every Peace loving person in this world would love to see a world of truly unconditional love. That beautiful state of being provides for a wonderful world view. We could actually live in a world of live and let live to say the least. This so inadequately describes what such a world can look like.

However, I trust that it is certainly within the imagination of the average person. For, we've just about all had visions of what we would call a utopia. Some other words used to describe this would be Paradise, Heaven on Earth, etc.... This doesn't seem to be the goal of those elites who run the world as designed the way it is today.

Why did this perpetuation of "conditional" love suit the needs of the elites of this world? Why did the elites of this world orchestrate such a depressing, bleak, and negative world that only serves the perpetuation of loneliness, insecurity, pain, misery, and suffering?

What are they getting out of such an evil mission? To understand that we need to open our minds and our willingness to accept and only reasonably scrutinize the field of study known as metaphysics. Because, in order to give this question proper investigation, we need to be able to understand in energetic terms, what is being produced and why is that valuable to anyone? Have you ever heard of energy vampires? No, I don't mean a character out of some Vincent Price horror movie. I am referring to those individuals who seem to always in or around situations that yield negative energy. These individuals who somehow seem to thrive off of this low vibrational energetic/ emotional output! Vibration and frequency have now been introduced into the conversation. Early on in our discussion, we touched on the meaning and scientific implications of vibration and frequency. We established that nothing in the known universe is completely at rest or still. Matter and energy alike are always in some form of motion and or vibration. This also applies to human energy and or emotion! Our every emotion or state of being have a vibrational frequency. Our energy output has a positive or negative charge or polarization to it ,like all energy. How is this negative energy created? In humans, it is most effectively produced by manipulating human emotion. This actually touches on a field of study accepted by mainstream science. Scientists have been successful at charting what human emotions correspond with a matching energetic stimuli. Many have produced vivid charts

depicting what vibrational frequency matches what human emotion. Frequency is the scientific measurement for the rate of how often something vibrates within a given time period (most usually per second). This is typically measured in a unit called hertz. Yes, folks this is still all within the framework of mainstream science. I haven't even started to delve into the metaphysical aspect of this. For now, we'll get back to those energy vampires. These are the kind of people who embody the age old saying " misery loves company"!

Energy vampirism is probably best described as a state of energetic dis-ease that manifests , in human beings as a form of deficiency. This deficiency is the prime motivating factor for the outward displays and the desperate behavior of a person who falls into this category. The energy vampire, when experiencing that deficiency, literally becomes desperate to satisfy that need or "hunger". It seems to only be satisfied by the absorbing of negative emotions, or in other words low frequency energy. Wow, now I'm starting to sound like a horror author! I wish! I wish that this was all just fiction! Unfortunately, the evidence proves that this is all to real folks! Please, never take my word as proof positive or anyone else for that matter. I always recommend that a person do research to verify and push back on any new information or school of thought. I could spend the next paragraph or even a page softening the blow or being less direct. Honestly, I don't think we can afford that! This should be shocking! We have been conditioned to and have blindly learned to not be shocked by the way this world has become. As a result, we have grown into a world of (let alone a nation of) lazy thinkers! We've become far too willing to just accept and believe. The elites of the world have done a frightfully effective job of grooming the world populous to be completely uninterested in doing the work that comes with seeking the truth or any form of growth! Essentially they have followed the age old and deviously efficient methods creating a slave race. Not just of one race of humans, but all human beings on the planet! Although, later we'll touch more on why highly melanated people have been most heavily targeted throughout history.

All the races of man have been controlled in a myriad of subtle and nefarious means. Sadly most of these means are and have been savage, vicious, heartless, low frequency, and hopelessly myopic! There simply are no relevant or important perspectives, other than that shared by the elite! At least, that's how they see it! So I ask, Are these the sort of individuals we would like to see dictating policy and law? No! Well then, let's view how they came to power. That effort should bring to light what path need be avoided, in order to avert such a terrible outcome. Since, the subjugation of the human species on this planet has been apparently going on for thousands of years, we have to go "back in time" again. We previously found ourselves in ancient Sumeria picking our way through that dark and sorted era in history. We've already started to see the most horrible side of human behavior, brought on by the curious desire to please a collection of temperamental, blood thirsty "deities". That provides us with (2) disturbed mentalities that we can begin to try to understand. I'm referring to that of the "needy" deities, and that of their eager subjects. It seems logical to start at the supposed "top of the hill" or should I say "top of the pyramid". An, Enlil, Ninhursag, and Enki, if they existed, must have made some form of contact with some group of early Sumerians. They must have influenced their initial human followers, in some way. Pathologically, we're searching for an origin or starting point for when people first started worshiping these " angry gods"! We can recollect many biblical stories that provide some source of "divine inspiration" helping us to understand why the people were inspired to follow. What's the motivation? Moses had the "Burning Bush", Noah had the "Divine Voice" directing him to build the Arch etc.... What was the event that initiated the onset of worship that demanded so much? What happened? To Whom? When? These are extremely difficult questions, as we traverse the rough waters of time, in search of answers! It would be much more than presumptuous to attempt to state any answers to those questions. Yet, many have speculated that likely there were some back then, who had some form of trance-like experience that provided some of the inspiration in question. What they are referring to would be very similar to the trance-like epiphany that Muhammad and other prophets were said to have experienced during revelation of different types. However, this is still just speculation. As with much of the history that we've peered through, we cannot be 100% certain of any of it! What we can do is objectively and intricately examine all the evidence available to us. The key word in the previously sentence is objectively. Then we apply that wonderful tool that our elders always used to point us to: COMMON SENSE. Most people have what some would call a natural "B.S." detector. Use It! Trust it! We're on dangerous ground where we don't "trust our gut" at all anymore! Just because an idea or concept is uncomfortable or difficult to "wrap your head around" doesn't mean it serves us to simply reject and ignore without investigation! This requires an open mind folks! So many of us, oddly much of the "scientific community", approach subjects that we're uncomfortable with a great deal of skepticism. Often, so much skepticism, that it at least partially hampers the scientific process of discovery! I am disappointed to say that this seems to happen to some of our most promising minds. We have all heard stories of how ancient mathematicians, scholars, explorers, and presumably enlightened individuals have been ridiculed, persecuted and often locked away in mental institutions for what was later found to be valid discoveries! This should tell us something of human nature, in dealing

with the unknown or difficult to believe! Don't be too alarmed, again, this is how we were groomed to be. Although, that in itself is alarming! Many people would shutter to think that man on a whole could be manipulated so deeply. Is our collective psyche really that fragile and easily impressed upon! Human beings on this planet have been victims to a multi-tiered mind manipulation that has been intricately developed and implemented over thousands of years. Yes, as unimaginable and frightening as that may be, we can't ignore the evidence for sake of feeling secure. the facts are the facts we need to get over the shock and mature as a species. It's time to take the next step in our evolution! That all important step has to be taken by freeing our minds! We simply must be a civilization of free thinkers and imaginative creators. That is the only way we can reshape our world in a way that serves our development, not that satisfies the insatiable hunger of the elites who've steered us all toward ruin! Now, that we've got the bad and ugly well covered (for now), we digress. Do you remember that very popular television series "The X Files"? Those two super sleuth-like characters Scully and Moulder were so entertaining in their adventures to uncover a secret government plot! Great for the ratings right?! However, in reality, most of the world's governments have, at some point, taken part in a "cover up" or "secret plot" that fuels the conspiracy theorists. I can leave them to it. The conspiracy theorists don't need my help. Instead I focus on asking those questions that linger in many of our minds that we try so hard to ignore. It seems to be necessary, for us to stay completely occupied, by the constraints of our daily lives. I need to ask, has anything ever been covered up by our or any other national government? Like for example, renewable energy?

Nichola Tesla was by most standards an unbelievably talented genius. He experimented with and eventually developed some incredibly groundbreaking technologies around renewable energy! Yet, this information has been held back and kept from the public for decades! Free energy models, "Zero Point" energy, anti-gravity, and mastery of magnetism list just some of Tesla's focus points! So, why would the world's governments suppress such valuable information. This is information on energy forms, and technologies that would drastically change the world as we know it. Yet again, why is there such an obvious effort by the world's elite to hide it all, and at all costs! Disappointingly, the issue at hand is $money$! Pause for just a moment to ponder, how the great breadth of dependence on fossil fuels handicaps our society as currently accessible energy forms are only being rationed out for a king's ransom. It is all to keep the world's elite in their constant positions of power. By controlling the world's resources and access to energy, these sick individuals are all but willing to see poverty, starvation, homelessness, pain, suffering and misery of the unsuspecting world populous to satisfy their own greed and unimaginable lust for power! Now, as we have begun to examine such character traits we are reminded of those early Sumerians who were manipulated into shedding their own humanity to appease "gods & deities" with

the same characteristics. In my mind, one thing is obviously missing in both situations.

That one incredibly important factor is Love! The power and positive energy that flows with true unconditional Love is vacant in either case! For, if their hearts were flooded with such a powerful wave of unconditional Love, we would not have to witness and bear the unfathomable amount of deprivation and negativity that we live in! A person with unconditional Love in their heart cannot just walk right past a homeless person sleeping on the street and not do something to help! Such a person could not just standby and watch as a child starves. A doctor with such Love in his/her heart cannot decide that one patient is more deserving of compassionate care than another. A teacher would never think that it's alright to favor one student while ignoring the developmental needs of another. A police officer would not be able to be violent with, or even kill an innocent unarmed citizen, yet serve and protect another. A judge could not harshly sentence and take away the freedom of one man/woman, yet fairly deal with someone convicted of the same. A leader of one country couldn't be alright waging a heartless violent war on another country's people, if they view them with the same value and compassion as they view their own people. Love wouldn't allow them to do it! That is why we must embrace a new way of life that accentuates truly unconditional Love! Now let's start to look at the broad concept of Respect. I mean Respect for all of our CREATOR's creations! Well, I guess we should first talk about why that is so important. That brings me back to concepts about energy, and our existence as energetic beings. We've established earlier that human beings are indeed energetic beings in physical bodies, since we concluded that humans are comprised of energy that is contained in a physical body consisting mostly of water and carbon. In fact, all lifeforms on Earth are physical bodies holding some form of energy! Science will tell you no different! Science will also verify that many physical forms are capable of holding different types of energy within them. Some very credible research has been done to establish that not only are many or perhaps all physical forms capable of containing energy, but consciousness or awareness, as well! This goes to somewhat support the plethora of theories out there on "group consciousness". Many fans of the popular R&B group "Frankie Beverly and

Maze" will remember their ever popular song "We are One". They "hit the nail on the head" with that one! In reality, all things at they're most simplistic form are energy. When energy is concentrated from a formless collection of atoms into material it becomes matter! Your mainstream scientists won't argue against this. At least, I don't think they will (HA HA). The point is that on a very basic energetic level all things in existence spring from the same source. Doesn't that mean that at least on some level we are all connected, given we share the same origin? Of course, we are! Therefore, "Frankie Beverly and Maze" had it right! We are all one! With that in mind folks, don't we all deserve a little respect? Think about your answer. Then ask yourself, "don't I deserve some respect?" Now, combine concepts! If we are all connected (all creations), then if one of us deserves a little respect, don't we all? Many would scoff at the idea of showing respect to a rock or tree! Most folks have enough difficulty showing respect to each other these days! Sad fact, huh? It would be very beneficial to our discovery to better understand why human beings have such difficulty in having respect for anything or anyone? A great example of this is our propensity to view other creations as less than or even subservient to us in some way. For those people, it is absolutely ridiculous to respect every person as an equal, let alone an "inanimate" object like a tree! However, please recall our previous scientific assurances that not only may all things potentially hold energy, but consciousness or awareness as well. For furtherance on the science of these concepts please independently research the work of Dr. Masaru Emoto. Dr. Emoto was born in Yokohama, Japan in July 1943 and a graduate of the Yokohama Municipal University's department of humanities and sciences with a focus on International Relations. In 1986 he established the IHM Corporation in Tokyo. In October of 1992 he received certification from the Open International University as a Doctor of Alternative Medicine. Subsequently he was introduced to the concept of micro cluster water in the US and Magnetic Resonance Analysis technology. Of course, there are others who have done studies in that field. You can always find more on the subject, if you may be thirsty for more scientific validation. Given this, can we still hold the opinion that the only beings or things worthy of our respect are ourselves? Here is where logic comes into play once again! Is it not logical that if we can verify that a plant has feelings, or a rock can vibration frequency and awareness. Of course it is logical, it has been proven! So, with that line of thought don't we in fact have a moral obligation to show all things some measure of respect? How about showing a little respect to our planet and all the wondrous creations that call it home!? I know, it sounds simple enough. However, man in general, has really struggled with this for literally thousands of years. Why? This brings us back to the very unfortunate, and down right ugly shaping of man's very psyche! Humans on this planet have been brain-washed, actually trained to think and behave this way. I touched on the early Sumerian civilization. Remember that, they built the empire-like city state of Babylon. Yet, there were many other early civilizations that fell into the same self centered, base, low vibrational psychotic mentality and behavior patterns. The point is that, sadly early man was lead astray! Even worse, our apparent fear of the unseen perpetuated this flaw in our collective mentality by leaving us susceptible to worshiping deities with the same flawed mentalities. Fear of the unknown drove us to organized religion. Here's where I'll lose many of my readers! In my humble opinion these religions have only compounded the problem, and left us even more flawed and fearful of the unseen. Many of the world's mainstream religions have made it completely taboo to even discuss such subjects! Then to make matters even worse, these religions openly preach distrust and vilifying of

other religions that differ from theirs, even slightly! I can remember, as a child, I was raised in a typical " Christian-Baptist" family. I was expected to attend church with the rest of the family. So I did. Yet, I never felt quite right about what I was hearing. At least, about some of it. A perfect example comes to mind. I can recall after Sunday school, I and some other children went with one of the church personnel to a grocery store. While in one of the isles we encountered a Muslim man with his traditional garb on. It didn't take the "church lady" long to start attempting to brainwash myself and the other children against this perfect stranger, who had done nothing wrong. At some point, she actually called this poor man a "devil-worshiper" who was destined to burn in "hellfire"! That sort of intolerance for other belief systems, is sadly typical! What may be, the worst part of this experience is that she showed no hesitation in inflicting this toxic mentality on unsuspecting children! This, in fact, is a microcosm of how intolerance and indifference has spread through even our most enlightened civilizations! There are very few exceptions. I think that it is very plain to observe, that such narrow ways to view the beliefs of others, has stained the civilization and development of our species. Yet, I would say that it is a product of our lack of respect for anything other than ourselves! Selfish doesn't begin to explain how man has behaved on this planet! We have not respected other people, let alone other animals or beings! Realistically, we've shown behavior that would send the message that we care not for our very planet! You know, come to think of it, humans are the only animals to destroy our own nest! Wow, think about that!!!

What does that say about us? Environmentalists have done an excellent job of documenting the terrible abuses we subject our beautiful Earth to. The very place of refuge, in the cold darkness of space that has been our home, we're actively destroying. Humans along with so many other beautiful species have flourished on this spectacularly picturesque place called Earth, a.k.a Terra. Logically, one would think we would value this planet. Yet, year after year we flood her oceans and other bodies water with obscene amounts of pollutants. We regularly do the same to her lands and atmosphere, with no remorse! The fact that we are mostly aware of the damage being done to our home and still can't stop is astounding! Indeed this behavior by any other species would be considered quite sick and deranged. It wouldn't be tolerated. However, we continue on, as though we're trying to see how close to the brink of extinction we can push it! You know "we do it". Humans, with the eventual advent of fluid space travel, will just settle another planet like this one. Then use it up until we throw it away like Earth! This insanity must stop! With such a sick mentality, would it even be good for us to have inter-stellar travel available to us? Wouldn't we be somewhat like the "scourge" of the universe? No wonder, we were depicted as such in the fairly recent version of "The Day the Earth stood still", starring Keanu Reeves. Before the end of the movie, he was able to see some positive potential in human beings. This gave him some hope for our future. I have that same hope and confidence that we can and will be better! That simply cannot happen without us all taking Michael Jackson's advice and looking in the mirror. We can only get on the right path by determining when and how we got on the wrong path. That is my aim, in writing this. I know we can do it we've all got to do our part. Hopefully, this and whatever else I can do aid us all in moving forward. I like to quote "Pops", one of the characters in the popular netflix show "Luke Cage". He always would say "remember Luke forward always forward!"

So, let's move forward, with hope. You can call me naive, but I still believe in the best qualities of people. Have you ever found yourself watching two puppies playing, thinking " they're just too cute"? Have you ever taken the time to stop and smell a flower? Have you ever woke up 1st thing in the morning taken a deep breath and proclaimed, " it's going to be a great day today!"? have you ever saw a baby bird fallen out of a nest and decided to help it out?Have you ever witnessed a young boy stop to help an old lady across the street, or a young girl help an elderly man? Did you find yourself smiling? Trust me folks! No matter how bad things have become, we have it in us to be incredibly compassionate and empathetic. Yes, there are still a lot of really good people in this world! As deep down as it may hide at times, we have it in us to be good hearted positive contributors. Our creativity can be shockingly inspiring at times. Although our history on this planet may appear murky, if viewed with an open mind and taking in all the factors, there's hope for us yet! We can look back at early civilizations like the DOGON tribes, the Yoruba people of West Africa, the Mayans and Olmecs of South

America and our "Native American" tribes who all lived in harmony with nature and were far more advanced and civilized than they've commonly been given credit for. Really people there's hope! Not all man has been so terrible for the planet. Man is capable of respecting this planet, its animals and resources etc... We simply must place a far greater value, nay love, on every aspect of our wonderful lives on this spectacular planet we have been blessed with! Most of us can and will change! It's going to require open mindedness, a lot of objective pathological thought and research. Above all , it takes the entire human race to be willing to do the work! I believe in us! Let's believe in us and get this done!

Chapter #2- Religions and Belief Systems

In chapter #1, we uncovered much, to say the least. We learned a lot about ourselves, our planet, and the direction that man has gone in his stewardship of the planet! We also learned about how we've behaved toward one another and our precious planet. We see now that we have a lot of growing to do still! So perhaps, it is very fitting that this chapter deal with two very important areas of potential growth: Religion and Belief Systems. In order to give our best effort in adequately covering this topic, we'll need to step back into our role as pathologists. We find that we'll need to once again become virtual time travelers to gain clarity on where we were, what we've done, what we've learned, and how that applies now. I'll first pose the question, what is religion? Religion in it's denotative definition is the belief in and worship of a superhuman controlling power, especially a personal God or gods forming a particular system of faith. A more practical meaning to many is organized group spirituality. However, the two are very different, Indeed! Religion provides man with a means of coping with his/her fear and lack of understanding for the unseen, on a group level. Who gives us this platform to cope with our very finite and limited means of comprehending such a vast and encompassing subject? To begin this journey, I think it would be helpful to look at what words and rituals we use in our religions, what they mean and where they come from. Remember, pathological thought! Let's start with the ever popular "Amen". This is probably the most often heard phrase in churches across the U.S. and the rest of the Christian world, but where does it come? Well folks, having grown up in a "Baptist" background, I can tell you that "Amen" the way "we" say it, has always had great importance. Especially when the pastor leads us to say it in unison. It is a very powerful tool to move the crowd! My, my, my, look at how the crowds have grown! We are not just sitting with our neighbors in a cozy setting hearing "the word" and enjoying fellowship. Now, we may have a small personable congregation or one as large as 50,000 members or more! That doesn't even account for the T.V. audience which might be in the millions! All of which sway and proclaim with perfect synchronicity ,when prompted to say "Amen"! What I find incredibly interesting is the fact that most of these folks have no idea what it actually means! The phrase "Amen" is derived from worship of the Kemetic (Egyptian) deity Amen Ra. Isn't it somewhat surprising that the most widely accepted monotheist religion in the entire world has from it's onset fully embraced a term that is in worship of a deity other than their beloved Jesus! If that leaves you wanting to find more of these curious links to ancient Kemetic (Egyptian) worship, many can be found throughout the modern version of the Bible. We have only to look at many of the story of Biblical characters like the ever popular Moses. He was actually a Hebrew child raised as a Kemetic prince, according to the story. How about

the traditional garbs worn by the clergy? They are rather ritualistic, right? Perhaps this connection to ancient Kemet comes from the Baptist Churches' link to the Catholic Church. Most of us grew up with a real denial or ignorance of any connection to the Catholic Church. However, this couldn't be further from the truth, once you consider that all Christian clergy are at some point trained in the Catholic Churches' Seminary! This and other ties are verified by similarities in things like the celebrating of Christmas on December 25th, the entire ritual procession of "communion",as well as some burial and funeral practices. Thus, while their are many, many divisions or sects of Christianity, all are simply compartments of the Catholic Church on a whole. There are even some undeniable connections between the "secret societies" previously discussed, and the Catholic Church! However, I will revisit that later.

I will not be going on into some theological lesson on the world's major religions. There are scores of volumes written on the subject. Why be redundant? Rather my job here is to highlight the connections. That takes me back to the Bible. The importance of this book, to Christianity, as a scripture, cannot be overstated! The Bible is the absolute authority and historical reference in Christianity, just as the Quran is to Islam. There are many other ties between the two. Having actively practiced both of theses major religions, I find myself having the perfect perspective. I am generally a fairly pious man. I take my spirituality and previously my religion, very seriously! I have been a rather devout member of both a Baptist Christian Church congregation and then later of a Suni Uma (Islamic congregation). I have in the past, opened my heart to true belief in both of these religions! I know what I'm speaking of directly on this! One need not look that deep into it, to see that prophet Muhammad, by many Suni Muslims is worshiped very similar to the way Jesus Christ is by Christians. The Nation of Islam, in my opinion, worships Elijah Muhammad just the same. Members of either Islamic sect or division, may deny this. However, remember I have an insider's point of view! I received my introduction to Islam through the Nation of Islam! Interestingly enough, while I have not been an active member of any other religions, I have studied several religions, to some degree. I have studied the basic theological foundation of Buddhism, Hinduism, Judaism etc... Truthfully, I have found far more in common among all of these religions, than differs. Yet, it is these few differences that are the fuel for disagreements, arguments, disparagement and even wars fought between religions! Once again man finds a way to transform what are essentially trivial points of separation into bloody conflict! Wait! I thought the whole purpose of these doctrines was to spread love and enlightenment to the masses through worship! Yet, somehow this is the opposite of what our experience with organized religion has been throughout history. Taking that into account, one would logically conclude that these religions have not just fallen short, but have failed! That obviously means humanity on a whole may need to turn toward other means of expressing and expanding awareness in spirituality. However, as billions

of people still worship in these religions, perhaps reform is the answer. Solving that problem is an ongoing struggle that is the responsibility of the leaders within those religions. For our purposes, we will need to focus on the impact of these doctrines, on the average person. One of the ways that the average "Joe/Jane" is heavily impacted is the inability to embrace and display true unconditional Love. Unconditional Love would need to be paramount in a religion for it to permeate the hearts and minds of its followers. Sadly, this simply is not the case in today's organized religions. Instead, the underlined message is that absolute conditions must be fulfilled, in order to receive the overwhelming love and acceptance of the "God" or deity that is being worshiped in the religion. There are rigid requisites for being considered a "Good Christian" or "Good Muslim" etc...How incredibly difficult must it be, to extend unconditional Love as a person,when the very Higher Power that you worship has a myriad of conditions that you must meet to appease that Higher Power or achieve the objective of your devoted worship? After all folks remember, he's a jealous "God", and he has wrath for the wicked or any whom do not follow the tenants of the religion they practice! Whoa! One better be careful!

Shouldn't religion build you up rather than break you down, in any way? If we cannot count on unconditional Love from our "God", where in this world can we get it? Is there any religion meeting its obligation to it's devout worshipers by teaching, preaching and extending unconditional Love to the masses, who yearn for it? I mean, think about the numbers for a minute. There are approximately 2.2 billion Christians and 1.8 billion Muslims, in the world. That's an estimated 4 billion people just between two religions. the impact of these mammoth congregations is undeniable. The impact of religion on the human psyche is ,therefore, something we cannot underestimate when examining the relationship between religions and humans seeking PEACE, LOVE, and RESPECT! Therefore, with such a vast reach of influence and devoted followers numbering in the billions, one can easily see how religion has indeed shaped our world! While this explains how religion has shaped our world, we can now ponder the purpose or aim of these religions that have become dominant Institutions in our lives!

That brings us to uncovering the earlier mentioned rituals and intricately detailed ceremonies. All, of the world's religions display very specifically executed ceremony and just as detailed garments to go along with them. These garments have profound meaning in all of these ceremonies, down to the design and color of these garments. Why such pomp and fuss? Why so such specificity? Why so many hidden meanings not disclosed to the congregations or Uma's? Likely, that is accounted for by the ties to those same ageless and mysterious "secret societies" mentioned in chapter one. Wait! What are the direct ties between the agenda of these secret groups representing the world's elite and the world's major religious bodies? Well, we've got to first recollect that the two dominant world religions are both impacted heavily by the world's most powerful

religious entity, the Catholic Church! Hold on, we've established that all Christian sects and denominations follow the lead of the Catholic Church in some way, shape, or form. Now, we are essentially stating the same of Islam! Yes, that's correct. Again, I can tell you from the inside that it's not really even all that hidden in Islam! Muslims are trained that their brothers and sisters in faith are Christians, and that the differences in the doctrines should only be pointed out to help rather than criticize. Perhaps, this is one of the main reasons why the Nation of Islam in America has historically caused rumblings throughout the world of Islam! The Nation of Islam would actually train its followers to be astute enough in both the Quran and the Bible as to be able to effectively debate Christians on site! I know this to be true personally! However, recent years have seen the current leader of the Nation of Islam, Minister Louis Farrakhan, steer them in a very different direction. He has openly embraced the Christians! He has established strong ties and relationships with many prominent Christian leaders. The most profound display of this new union is the practice embraced by Min. Farrakhan and his followers, of referring to the CREATOR as God! He and his team of ministers, teachers and speakers have just about all done this! This is not just some weird coincidence of whimsical change. This is a purposeful change and veers away from the previous doctrine put forth by Elijah Muhammad! Elijah Muhammad would often say "Allah or God", to ease a predominantly Christian audience to be open to actually hearing the entire speech to get the message. Now, the surface explanation given for this is that it was done in the pursuit of unity and in aiding the "black" community. However, I question that. Why? Because, for a religious organization with such conviction to paying homage to Elijah Muhammad, they have strayed pretty far in this area! So, Why has this happened? Does this demonstrate the apparent ties between organized religion and the "Belief Systems" of the secret global organizations, earlier mentioned? Well, that brings us back to the colors and meticulously designed garments worn in the ceremonies of the Nation of Islam, and other religious organizations. One can't help but to take note of the black and red uniforms of the "Fruit of Islam", or think something is suspicious about the similarities between the garments worn by the Women of the Nation of Islam and Catholic Nuns, minus the desert head wrap of course! The ties are undeniable! Secret societies or organizations have long been obsessive about ceremonial garbs and strict adherence to using the colors red and black. Is it because these colors hold a potentially dark meaning spiritually? The decorations on these garbs and head wear, often adhere strictly to the use of sacred geometry or "geomatria", by these secret societies. Why does this show up in Christian and Islamic worship alike? Again, we are left to conclude that this is simply further evidence of ties between these major religions and these secret societies! Yet, we have not yet uncovered substantial and undeniable proof of such connection to the Catholic Church. Well, this is where I should be offering a blue or red pill right? Isn't this where we have to decide for ourselves whether or not to go down the rabbit hole? We've got to ask ourselves how much do we want to know? How badly do we want to know it? We must decide if we are comfortable just existing in this paradigm, or do we absolutely need the truth? I suppose you could just shut the book, right now! However, I don't think you're much of a "scaredy cat", or you likely would have never picked up this book,in the first place. So, let's stay on this mission together, and let's dive right in, like Kendrik Lamar into his "Swimming Pools"!

To start with, we should at least have a rudimentary understanding of the most widely known, yet mysterious, secret organization to most people. Of course, I'm referring to Masonry and the newly popular to discuss "Illuminati". The "Illuminati" are a little too debatable to serve our purpose here. At least, for now! That means we should unveil what we know of the Masonic Orders. I think more specifically, we have a lot to learn about the deeply symbolic ritual of striving toward the masonic accomplishment of attaining 33degrees. It has been revealed that there is a very symbolic ceremony where the individual must traverse a long hallway with 33doors. Obviously this is symbolic of the process of attaining 33degrees. First, we need to ask, what is the symbolic significance of the33 doors in this long hallway. The 33 doors actually symbolizes the 33 vertebrae in a human spinal column! The opening process of these 33 doors, is that it represents the "Kundalini" awakening. The Kundalini is said to be a human's raw spiritual energy and direct connection to the powerful human spirit! The Kundalini energy must travel up all 33 vertebrae to find its way through the base of the skull to reach the "Pineal Gland". Wait, doesn't that sound familiar? Yes, we've already talked about the importance of the "Pineal Gland" in chapter 1. Although, we have not discussed the apparent ties to the Catholic Church. Let's start with the Pope's staff. Near the top is a pine cone looking structure or symbol, that stands for the Pineal Gland. In the Vatican, stands a huge statue of a Pineal Gland! This statue is perhaps the largest in the entire complex. This further indicates the incredible importance of the Pineal Gland to the Catholic Church! What about the fact that most members of these secret societies are Christians! The majority of the rest are Muslims! Wait, I thought that these two Religions have been at war for centuries, if not millennia? Right, but who profits from wars? Remember that we've already uncovered the incredibly vast reach and influence of the secret societies! Allow me to lay this all out. These organizations recruit from birth, as the members are almost always sure to enlist their own families! That's right it's no fluke, when little Johnny is groomed (indoctrinated) from childhood to talk, act, think, and believe a certain way. Then Johnny is sent to private elementary school, then private middle school, and private high school, all pre-approved by these secret societies! Then Johnny is accepted into a prominent Ivy League University, also pre-approved! This is where the actual initiation into a secret society begins! Whether it's into a "Greek" Fraternity , or "Skull and Bones" or some other pre-approved recruiting arm. This gives Johnny his way into some of the most powerful fortune 500

companies, in the world! At some point along the way, he's invited down to the local Lodge, for his actual initiation! Now, throughout his life, he follows the "big picture" agenda of the secret society that has recruited him! That's just one example of how our brightest youth are swooped up by these groups in such subtle, undercover ways, never even noticed by the average person or even most members of his own family! The tentacles of these frighteningly cold calculating, methodical, and down right evil organizations extend into every aspect of our lives, with virtual invisibility! After all, it only takes a hand shake! So, Johnny (or maybe even your child) is sent to work in some of the very nefarious corporations who will then go unnoticed as they produce the "weapons of war", or reap the benefits of these wars in some other behind the scenes way! Do you remember all the U.S. oil companies who flooded into the Middle East, after the war in Kuwait? Oh, I almost forgot, many folks didn't know anything about that! How about our politicians? Many of them had to be complicit, to pull this stuff off over and over again. Let's not forget that most of them have been recruited along the way, as well! It's said that every U.S. President is a Mason!, Hmm! The ties are most certainly undeniable, even though I definitely have not supplied you with them all. I'll leave the rest to you, in your independent studies. Remember, never just rely on my words, or anyone else's word! Folks, our world is saturated with corrupt Religions and Belief systems. They're reach and influence permeates every school, home, relationship, and every Institutional aspect of our lives! What are we going to do about this! We'll certainly need to develop new Belief Systems replacing these corrupted World Religions first!

Chapter#3 New World Governments for a New World

It's Time Folks! We cannot deny that it's time to reshape this misshaped world. We have uncovered how far off the path of PEACE, LOVE & RESPECT we've gone. It is also very important to not forget that we (human beings) may not be entirely responsible! In fact, with what we've unveiled so far, it is safe to say that we can place blame or better yet responsibility squarely on the shoulders, of this world's elite. We are now being governed in accordance with the needs of the "Few", rather than the needs of the "many", as "Mr. Spock" would say! Yet somehow, we've found ourselves having fallen victim to the cross-generational plans of the "Military Industrial Complex", that Eisenhower tried to warn us all about! They have infiltrated every aspect of our society, nay our civilization on a whole! The way they've done this so shrewd and efficient, that it could be admired, if not so detestable! Perhaps, we wouldn't even mind if it weren't so evident how sick and demented their system of rule truly is! Now, we must begin examining, in some detail, how we let this happen. How did they pull this off right under our noses? I get the impression that, the fact that they have so largely fooled us, is something that they derive a great deal of pleasure from! After all, wouldn't that only play towards their apparent and gross arrogance? Even, Ralph Nader made some comments scratching the surface on the ominously stealthy "Military Industrial Complex" and how far reaching the influence of their power really is! Every now and then there's even a representative from the financial head of this complex, the International Banking System (domestically the "Fed") , who are bold enough to just come right out and say that they typically don't assert their influence on world governments unless those governments propose something that is not aligned with their agenda!" This is, in no uncertain terms, an open admitting of the fact that they essentially have Veto power over our government. Therefore, the folks you send to Washington, D.C. to represent you are actually representing the best interest of this nefarious "Military Industrial Complex". No wonder the world has suffered to see so many devastating wars! The few folks who actually "run the world", are the same people who make all the money from those wars! Through the years, there have been scores of folks, who have done their best to warn us all about this. Recently, Bernie Sanders used the floor of the U.S. Senate to make a passionate speech demanding that the fraud of the "Military Industrial Complex" and it's far reach be brought to an end! Almost ten years ago, Rep. Tim McDermott tried to warn the U.S. that the country's "Medical Industrial Complex" is even

larger than the "Military Industrial Complex"! What's way past alarming, is the fact that our Federal Government through the years has empowered the monstrously giant pharmaceutical industry to almost no end over the past 50 or so years! Evidence of this shows up plainly in the waves of questionable drugs that have "hit the market by storm" earning so much, so quickly that even when the law suits start, the producers can withstand the "hit" of liability and still make huge amounts of money! What has aided this greatly is the so-called "FDA fast track" used by these slick pharmaceutical companies! HG.org legal resources reports that the drug Nuplazid made its way to the market by taking advantage of the Food and Drug Administration's (FDA) "fast track" approval system known as "Breakthrough Therapy." This system is designed to speed up the FDA approval process for new forms of treatment based on minimal clinical data. Nuplazid was granted the Breakthrough Therapy designation after only a small amount of data was presented that the drug was more effective at treating psychosis in Parkinson's patients then other medications currently on the market.
However, a short time after Nuplazid hit the market, a large number of serious side

effects began to be reported by patients and caregivers. This has called into question whether the fast track FDA approval process is safe. Many patients and caregivers say they were not warned about the dangerous side effects of Nuplazid and have decided to file Nuplazid lawsuits. The NCLS (National Conference of State Legislatures) reports that in 2016, the United States spends more than $320 billion dollars on prescription medicines annually. Total spending on drug therapies is about $371 billion dollars, including over-the-counter (OTC) drug remedies, valued at 31 billion. All this, in an environment that pharmaceutical companies complain is profit restrictive for these "Pharma-Giants". Really! Let's ask some of those unfortunate people who found out the "hard way" about the crooked loopholes that these companies have wiggled through at their expense. Perhaps, we should ask some of the elderly citizens who have a tough time affording enough food to eat, because they can't keep up with the exponentially rising cost of their medications! Often increased 10 times or more, virtually overnight! I have personally met and spoke with many such folks right here in Western Pennsylvania. Some of these once proud, retired, working class folks have to eat dog or cat food, because it's cheaper!!! Where is the dignity and justice in that? Industry reps. generally offer no reason or supposed justification for the sharp price increases. In my opinion, the pharmaceutical industry doesn't care much about anything other than profit. At least not any more than the "gun industry", or any other industry that clearly seems to completely ignore such concerns, en route to the big bucks!

Another industry that has been permitted to almost completely ignore the well being of the citizens of this nation, is the Agricultural Industry. I have to go no further than the notorious previous Agri-giant corporation Monsanto corp. I say previous because, it has been recently announced that they've merged with (wait for it!) pharmaceutical giant Bayer. This comes only after they have been given the "green light" to experiment on the unsuspecting citizens of this nation, for the past 30-40 years or so! That's right these are the folks who were nice enough to share genetically engineered foods with us!

Some may argue that they've helped us by finding viable solutions to possibly ending hunger. However, hunger hasn't come close to being brought to an end, in fact it's increasing (that may be partially attributed to "terminator seeds"! I, for one, could never ignore the litany of health side-effects (many of which still being discovered) that we and our future generations have to live with. Nor, can I ignore the undeniable impact that these reckless corporations and other under-regulated Agri-corps. have had in our grocery stores! We can scarcely find any food that has a normal/healthy ingredient list, rather than what amounts to a list resembling what you'd find in a chemistry set! No wonder they merged with Bayer! Folks, aren't we supposed to be protected from this by the FDA. If not why does our tax money go toward keeping this lack luster, under performing, and down right corrupt Federal Agency in place? What about the EPA? Well, first let's clear this up now! Chemtrails do exist! There's no profound debate to be had. They are right there, in the skies above your and my neighborhood almost daily! Especially, in the summer months. Multiple environmentalist groups have effectively charted and compiled lists of toxins and soft metals that fall to waterways, crops, and on animals from these "fake clouds"! Once again, there is a plethora of evidence out there for any, who are not too lazy to look! What about the A.M.A.(American Medical Assoc.) who have turned a blind eye to this knowing the adverse effects on our collective health! Perhaps, they've had their own wicked experimental agenda? Haven't they essentially worked "hand in hand" with the pharma industry? What about the A.D.A.(American Dental Assoc.) Haven't they been pushing fluoride on us for decades? Fluoride is one of the worst toxic, narcotic, dangerous substances known to man! The Nazi's made great evil use of it on their prisoners in concentration camps! It's not only in our toothpaste and oral rinses, but it's being added to our drinking water along with toxic chlorine! Did they basically just take the playbook straight from those Nazi fiends? Oh wait, I almost forgot they did give safe haven to those awfully nice Nazi "Dr.'s" and "scientists". Don't take my word for anything! There have been 'whistle blowers' from every walk of life or level of government, over the past 40-50 years. We can only surmise that they have largely been ignored by most of us. What we should find insulting is the way it is completely taken for granted that we are simply the sheep who will follow whatever shepard they decide to put in front of us! Then again, how surprising is that when you consider that you've been programmed to just ignore and dismiss any of these questions and facts as "conspiracy theory" or " just crazy talk" right? However, the most dangerous element of this is that they have been able to control and dictate to our world governments, with virtual ease! Come on you beautiful and intelligent people, WAKE UP! I feel like early Spike Lee, in book form! Do you remember that great

man-up question, "are you mice or men/women?" Well folks which is it? We cannot allow this to continue! It's not up to some helping hand to come down from the sky! It's up to us! I can only speak for myself, but they've raised the man in me, or maybe the divine in me!

So, what must be done? How can we put forth a "herculean effort" to take back our world governments, or simply tear them down to get back to the proverbial drawing board and start fresh with "New Governments for a New World"? As with all true liberation efforts, first we must free our minds! Then we take action! We don't hesitate to take the kind of socially conscious action that will bring the kind of change, that is deserving to the unsuspecting masses of good people, who have been so savagely lead to ruin! They are worthy of a life of PEACE, LOVE, and RESPECT! To be clear, I am in no way calling for violence! The taking of a life or harming of any life is never a solution, just often the result of desperation, frustration and vengeance! What we need is to harness ideas! We have to learn to embrace the brilliance, and natural determination of our youth ,instead of constantly suppressing their ideas, like the ideas of so many brilliant minds of the past have been! I mean minds like that of the "not-often-enough" mentioned Nichola Tesla. His incredibly bright and innovative ideas on "free energy"/ "Zero Point" energy alone would have changed this world immensely for the better! Imagine a world not dependent on fossil fuels, the perpetual destruction of this beautiful planet and the subjugation of the "third world". We could open our minds to natural and holistic medicine freeing us from our dependence on these toxic drugs and experimental "medications" that are continually pushed on us. We can find sustainable cyclical forms of technology, rather than these uncivilized forms of destructive linear technology, we're so addicted to today! Rather than this current push for more and more artificial intelligence we should be pushing forward in expanding human intelligence and awareness! We should gain better understanding of and expansion of our spirituality! These solutions are already at our fingertips! We just have to not be too lazy to look! So let's take a peek at some of the past forms of government that we have already established, have failed us. Then with free thinking pathological minds, let's propose some potential new forms of government that would truly serve us all! Many early civilizations lived under a Monarchy. They embraced life in a society run by a ruling class, or more specifically a ruling family of royalty. We also see some ancient societies living in Dictatorships. In this form of government we see an individual ruler, much like the Nazis with Hitler as their unchallenged ruler and head of the ruling party. We've also seen countries living under Totalitarianism, Fascism, Republicanism, Democracy, Oligarchy, Socialism, and Marxism etc... Then, of course, there's the ever popular Communism! We see famous examples of this in China and the nation State of Cuba. All of these countries undoubtedly should be given credit for substantial contributions to the world's development. However, all at some point have stumbled into

the painful folly of war! They have all at some point seen their citizen's suffer and struggle to survive the devastating and crippling effects of war! Then, after the incredible toll of massive loss of life, untold suffering, and widespread destruction, it's the poor citizens of these lands that are left to pick up the pieces and rebuild. Most of us cannot imagine the macabre scenes of the aftermath of war! Yet, we really must envision this to appreciate the horror, from which we spring and wish never to return! I struggle with a heavy heart to visualize deceased men, women, and children's bodies being pulled from rubble by devastated and nearly broken survivors! All of this pain, shockingly is within the cold worldwide agenda of the "Elites" that have long considered the average person just "collateral damage". I am convinced that this type of callus manipulation and willingness to sacrifice the happiness and the very lives of the many, for the wants of the few, is the root cause of our history filled with vicious wars! We must change this deeply corrupted perspective of leadership in our "World Governments". Obviously that calls for not only a change of mind, but a serious change of heart! So, what we must change is "Separation". I am referring to "Separation" as a concept or mentality. Let me elaborate a little. I touched briefly on the concept that all beings and all things are made of energy. All energy in the universe essentially springs from the same source. Thus, all this energy is connected on some level. If we are all energy, and all energy is connected, then we are all connected, in some way. This lends itself to a mentality that views all people,and all things as being interdependent and all impacting all, through "Cause and Effect". Therefore, if I am of this mentality, I see that my actions do in some way impact others and the"whole", in general. I then have to take ownership of all of my decisions and actions, knowing that there are always implications outside of my "sphere of reality". This is a basic understanding of what we call "Unity Consciousness" . This mentality doesn't allow for reckless decisions and actions that may negatively impact others, and/or the "Whole". Thus anyone of this mentality becomes far better suited to lead with the well being of all they lead in mind! This is the opposite of "Separation Mentality", where one only appreciates and considers all life situations from a purely self-centered perspective. It is that type of mentality, that we see in the minds of those who propagate the agenda of the "ruling elites" of this world! To establish truly effective, and comprehensively compassionate "World Governments", we need to embrace " Unity Consciousness" and denounce "Separation Mentality"!

Chapter # 4 Our Society Changes-

Now that we've learned so much together, what direction do we see "Our Society" heading in? What sort of changes should we expect? How will they be applied to our everyday life? First, let's recall that before we can hold anyone else accountable, we must hold ourselves accountable! We cannot afford "major slips" and "backtracking". We have to bring our progress to our individual families. We need to teach and/or re teach our children this new "Way of Life". Remember our children are quite literally our future! Even if we begin to do a good job of holding our governments accountable, it is our children that must continue this, so that a lasting pattern can be established. Then we have to break out of our comfortable little shells to regain a sense of real community. "Nice" areas that have almost grown as cold and detached, as the corporations that most of their successful residents work in, must regain that neighborly warmth and concern! Areas that are considered "hoods" have to now be valued, supported and turned back into neighborhoods! We must realize that our communities are the microcosm of our cities. Our cities are the microcosm of our states. Our states are the same to our Country. Our country the same to our continent. Continent to hemisphere, hemisphere to planet and you get the picture, I'm sure! However, let's not lose sight of the fact that none of this progress takes place without the change to the individual! That rounds us back to some previously covered topics. We need to diagnose, what are the most important factors in this individual change? What are the prescribed catalysts for such change? What does the average person today need, to point them undeniably in the right direction? What will keep them on target?

Maybe, we should start by looking at the obstacles that stand to block, or derail, individual mental/spiritual progress! Honestly, does it even make sense to assume that we would even make any progress with the forces that have held us back, still in place? Yes, because we can start to breakdown or better understand what is actually in place to affect individual progress? Once we correctly diagnose that, we can decipher how to counteract it! What in our lives impacts our psyche on a daily basis? How about our t.v. and/or cell phones (devices). We pay more attention to these sources of input and stimuli, on a moment to moment basis, than just about anything else in our lives! So what are we getting from them? One thing that we are constantly bombarded with is advertisements. Have you ever wondered why companies spend such staggering amounts of money on advertising? Psychology! The people who specialize in coming up with the plethora of multi-media ads, that we are attacked with unrelentingly, rely on psychology! You may be saying to yourself "come on attacked is kind of harsh isn't it?" However, the general method of these sneaky ads is to create and accentuate

insecurity, in our minds! To quote Kanye West, "we're so insecure"! What a great way to create the business necessity of "demand"? The most important concept to all businesses is supply and demand. Thus, any business can be as successful as they want to be, if they can actually manipulate our psyche to constantly create demand! All they have to do, after that, is supply! Essentially, the plan is to flood all multi media with ads that inflict subtle damage to our ego (which we rely on far too much), to instill the thought that there's something about us that needs fixed! We are trained, by all this well disguised "psycho-warfare" to question everything about ourselves. This has developed an entire world of insecure people with an intense need to fill the hole that is created in our psyche, by these sneaky negative ads. The unsuspecting victims of these attacks seek desperately to fill this hole with material possessions, body alterations, and attention diverting devices. How many of us look in the long mirror and are unhappy or even depressed about what we see? How many of us emphatically must have a certain level of wardrobe/fashion to be happy? How many of us are absolutely obsessed with having the newest best looking car, whether we admit to ourselves or not that it's to grab attention? How many of people walk around all day with their attention completely diverted by the cell phone or device that they just can't look away from? All of this perpetuates a sick cycle, that erodes the person's ability to appreciate themselves, as they are, without all those superficial fixes! Thus, self-love becomes nearly impossible, for a person who suffers in this way! If you don't truly love yourself unconditionally, you don't have it within you to love someone else unconditionally! Unfortunately, "Our Society" is saturated with negative stimuli that has this devastating effect! Again, this is another way that we are playing right into the hands of the elites! Why do you think they call the T.V. the "idiot box". Decades ago, they came up with a notorious invention called the "Brunswick" T.V. The "Brunswick" T.V. was said to be utilizing a then experimental form of subtle "mind control" technology. The average unsuspecting consumer was essentially experimented on! These T.V.'s and other similar devices utilized manipulation of the electro-magnetic waves emitted by the T.V.'s, during certain specific "progamming", that was designed to use subliminally suggestive stimuli to inspire these consumers to react to the advertisements by purchasing products from certain commercials, even if they didn't need the products at all! This is just one small example of early "brainwashing" and or "mind controll" techniques. There is even a modern U.S. Patent #6,506,148 for this technology!!! The inventor credited is Mr.Hendricus G. Loos. There is a description given by the U.S. Patent office that reads "It is therefore possible to manipulate the nervous system of a subject by pulsing images displayed on a nearby computer monitor or TV set. For the latter, the image pulsing may be embedded in the program material, or it may be overlaid by modulating a video stream."

-- US Patent and Trade Office, Patent #6,506,148 on subliminal behavior modification, 1/14/2003 . Once again good people, do not take my word for it. Simply look up U.S. Patent #6,506,148! We are living in a country where corporations are given virtual free reign to use such sickening, invasive, and down right evil tactics to manipulate our minds technologically, just to make more money! Yes, the insatiably greedy elites of this world actually want you to suffer, in this way! It makes them money! Not to mention, the ever important, behind the scenes, even more nefarious reasons given earlier! One thing for sure, they are not creating an environment that is conducive for "Unconditional Love". You can recall that the lack of true "Unconditional Love" is one of our worst obstructions. It stands in the way of progress toward PEACE, LOVE, and RESPECT! So, in order to move forward with a truly "Changed Society", we must take the initiative to derail these detestable technologies! We have to educate ourselves on what's really happening in our world! We must eliminate the apathy within ourselves that is satisfied with going through our lives being obsessed with material gain and get our focus back on protecting what really matters! That's us! Don't we owe that much to our children? Can we afford to be distracted so easily? If we don't take action to change ourselves on an individual basis, what sort of future will we be leaving for our children and future generations? These questions are not just rhetorical, each person needs to find the answers for themselves! It is only through each individual changing for the better, that we will set off that chain reaction I described earlier in this chapter! Don't we need to? Well, great news folks! I am more than hopeful. I am confident that the chain reaction has already begun! I see evidence in this everyday as I interact with more and more people who genuinely surprise me, in the best way! I derive the most gratification when I observe this in our young adults! Everyone, it's time to stop putting down this marvelous generation! We have to hold them up, and help them out! They are our future leaders, and the future is here! Now, let's get out of their way and let them lead! They can do it! We can all do it together! Please don't forget, WE ARE ONE!

Chapter# 5 Families-

For most people, there is nothing more important in this world, than family! The great majority of folks define themselves and the life they live, through family! Family relationships can most certainly be some of the most beautiful that a person, may have! I consider myself particularly blessed in this area. I have had the incredibly rewarding and fulfilling experience of raising an unbelievably beautiful family with a truly special partner (Regina). She and I have three(3) children together, two(2) handsome boys (Daniel & Osei) and one(1) beautiful girl (Aisha). They are now adults aged 26,22,and 20. Their mother is one of the sweetest, warmest, brightest and generous persons I have ever met! I will love her forever! Our children are so wonderful to me that I truly struggle to adequately describe my undying love for them! Mere words simply fall very short of expressing how much they mean to me! My face floods with tears of joy at any opportunity to take a moment to ponder the unimaginable depth of my love and appreciation for them! I know now that it is only the capacity given me by OUR CREATOR (Higher Power) to encompass such a degree of unconditional love! As with all things, I am truly unfathomably grateful to OUR CREATOR, for that love! I just realized that throughout this book, this is the first time I even mentioned my gratitude toward OUR CREATOR! While, it is true that I am in no way religious, I am very,very spiritually aware. While I acknowledge no deity or god as a supreme being, I cannot even attempt to capture my love for MY CREATOR , with words. So, I won't try. I will only state that I know, without doubt, that all things flow from one(1) truly eternal SOURCE! I flow oh so gratefully from that SOURCE!

In this world, we have the tendency to qualify our love for one another. I've already talked a lot about how we place conditions on our love. True Love requires no qualifications nor conditions! That's what Unconditional Love is all about! We can only truly access that Love through OUR CREATOR. He/She blesses us with Unconditional Love for our family. It is something that, in general, we don't have to work at. If we are blessed to have a close family, we have that Love from the time we enter our family! Unfortunately, the negative influences of this world often pull apart and fragment our families and we just call it life! Why? How do we suffer such separation and loss, in so many ways? How does this world erode the many, many beautiful bonds that connect us to our "Families", so intimately? Why would we ever allow this? Do we even notice? I think, we usually do not until it has already happened! We can't overstate the impact of us constantly being distracted with the "rat race", of everyday life in our present day society. It seems that, it would be a great benefit for anyone to be successful at finding

a viable way to separate ourselves from the infamous "rat race". Perhaps, then one would be a lot more capable of preventing themselves from ever losing sight of the things that truly matter most in our lives, rather than the material and superficial things that we tend to replace them with in our subconscious hierarchy of importance! I know I just said a mouthful, but ponder that for a minute. Then take a moment to think about your life and what you value most in it! Being a very spiritual person, I find it apparent that OUR CREATOR supplied us with that innate sense of family and unconditional love for them, for a profound reason. Therefore, far be it for me to ever undervalue that! Instead, I will cast a "shadow of doubt" on this cold world's indoctrination that has conditioned us to feel differently, about our Families. I talked earlier about the difference between the true Unconditional Love and the co-dependency that we find ourselves developing. I think that we tend to veer down the path of co-dependency with our Families subconsciously, in efforts to cope with this cold world we find ourselves in. I think that we do this because we put so much energy and faith into these flawed religions that cause us to feel separate, from OUR CREATOR! We often think and or feel that we are only connected to Source, when we are in some house of worship(church, temple, mosque, or synagogue etc...). Thus, we dependently latch onto the only source of Unconditional Love available to us in this world! For most, that is our Families. Sadly for some family isn't even an option. How sad must be the orphan child, who can't help but to think " no one wants me, because no one loves me!" Many of us have heard the old saying that "it takes a whole tribe to raise one child". At some point in our past, and in some ares of this world, we actually practiced that. That type of extended family value, truly leaves no child behind. I think that would be beautiful to get back to. For now, these precious young people with so much potential to offer are left behind as wards of "The State" or discarded as an unwanted burden. We must change this! Every child has unlimited value! No child is worthless! If we are successful at our endeavor to revive and re-establish true Unconditional Love, This to, we will fix! When we remain dependently rooted in our immediate family bubble, we lack the vision or ability to embrace even our extended families let alone those in need whom we sadly consider outsiders (even though they are in need)! The very unfortunate result of this is often that we overcompensate with our immediate family members. How many parents find themselves proclaiming " my child won't have to want for anything!" What we are actually teaching is that life is about chasing your wants, rather than satisfying your needs. The separation, from those outside family, that we develop while overcompensating causes us to subconsciously allow our hearts to chill towards the average person in need(outsiders)! How many of us, and how many times have we stepped over or walked right by another human being who is downtrodden, broken (in pain) and homeless? Even if it's freezing cold outside and that person is sleeping on a cold, cold sidewalk, do we still just pass by indifferently? How cold hearted, as a society,

have we truly become? Perhaps, it is reversible, if we can re instill Unconditional Love into our hearts?

When I was maybe 10 or 11 years old, I remember one morning before school listening to my Father's "CB radio" and hearing truckers over the air cracking all sorts of racist jokes about Black people! I can revisit, in my mind, the raw feelings of hurt and anger bubbling in my heart and mind! When I went to school that day I think I had my first day of feeling prejudice and or racism! I had always been taught to love myself and my people, and others equally! I was taught that, despite racist people, I should not be racist myself. I had no problem with this, as my nature as a young boy was to be forgiving and loving. However, something was different that day. I walked the halls of my school (Linton Jr. High Penn Hills, PA) feel something akin to pure hatred toward the white students and teachers. I had heard white people spewing racist comments before, but somehow this was different! That morning, I had the kind of revelation that a young boy shouldn't have to process. It gave the sobering and angering thought that "this is what they really think of us". From that point on through my early adulthood, I began to embrace the conflict between Black and White people. While I never took a life or seriously injured anyone in reaction to this, I did engage in racially motivated fighting, bullying and other deeds I am not proud of today. This really wasn't my true character. I had developed the "gangsterfied" identity of "Ease Dawg". Since, I had become a custom to violence in general, fighting white people (whom I had come to regard as all racists) was a natural choice. When my Father died I had just turned 13 years old! I still feel the shock and pain of losing my best friend, in the world! My Father and I hadn't always been so close! So, when he died I felt like he was stolen from me just when I was beginning to enjoy our relationship the most! After a life of battling alcoholism (like so many inner-city black folks), he had succumb to lung cancer! I guess the good thing I got out of that pain, was NO desire to smoke! I followed the typical troubled youth path, from there on. I regressed from an "A-B" student to failing most of my classes. However, somehow I managed to barely graduate, in 1991. I even attended Community College of Allegheny County, for a few years. Although, even that couldn't keep me out of the trouble I had grown comfortable with. I soon committed an armed robbery and was sentenced to 2-4 years in a Pennsylvania State Penitentiary. That's the first time I recall feeling like a slave. Most notably, when I first took a look at my meager paycheck at the rate of .43 cents/per hour! That feeling would come and go throughout my sentence. Even though I had refused to see any family, when I was at "Camp Hill" for classification, my family stood by me! While incarcerated, I had been exposed to teachings from a multitude of sources, some I was already familiar with. Once released, I was quite different. I had some incredible experiences of self reflection. I had an epiphany and found myself far more spiritual than I had ever been, in any religious setting. After re-adjusting to society and becoming a "family man", I grew even more spiritually. I then had some very profound experiences (like watching my children born) that expanded my spirituality further. I also had some very unexpected experiences in interacting with white folks, that altered me still! I am now able to look back on my life and notice some of the positive ways that other races of people have impacted my life experiences. I have a far more tempered and wise perspective that comes with maturity and spiritual growth. That growth can and needs to be embraced by us all, but it is possible, only through Unconditional Love. Then with that growth, we can reach past the artificial boundary lines of insecurity, mistrust, and paranoia that hold us back from embracing all people, all animals, and all things with love! Again, I believe in the good, in people of this world. I am confident that we can push forward to a time on this planet when we can extend our extended Families to include all! I know sounds "corny" and idealistic, Huh? I assure you folks we can and will get there! Yet, we cannot expect to accomplish this without putting in the work! Please remember the "chain reaction". All we have to do is put this in motion by initiating that first spark of self change, growth, and expansion! We will accomplish this by expanding our consciousness and opening our hearts to such a beautiful and profound change! Then we will expand our scope of what we consider Families, and then the new Human Family will be born!

Chapter #6 - "An End to Miseducation"

The only reason that most of what we've uncovered is so surprising, is that we were not exposed to this information. Imagine, a new paradigm where all children have free access to grow up in an educational system that offers not only a challenging curriculum, but one that does not hold back the truth from it's students. The thought of that should be pleasing, to just about any parent. Unfortunately, that's not the agenda of the elites of this world! Why? How does suppressing truth maintain the world vision of these elites? What is the danger in a world of intelligent, pathological, free thinking people with access to unlimited sources of objective information? What lengths, will these elites go, to prevent this reality? Perhaps, the better question is what have they already done. Why have we not been taught some very basic information about ourselves and our physical bodies. For example, the pineal gland is a major component of the endocrine system in the human body, yet most people walking around today have no idea what it is! Why would such a prominent gland in our bodies go virtually uncovered in school curriculum nationwide? Why, would melanin be passed off as a mere skin pigment, when it is one of the most complex molecules known to man and is in all beings at some concentration and is found in every cell of people with a very high concentration of melanin (dark skinned races)? This should be taught to every student in every classroom! However, we find that most schools and classrooms suffer not only from revisionist history, but selective access to some of the most important facts about our physical bodies! Why? It takes a lot of work to omit such important things, and to even take steps to ensure that these facts are not uncovered! So obviously, there is something about that information being known widespread, that makes this world's elite very nervous! I recently watched some old episode of some "Star Trek-like" T.V. series where a species of humanoid beings were desperate to replenish their vastly diminished numbers. To do this they needed to usurp the DNA code and genetic material of a more primitive species of humanoids. Since the more primitive humanoids held far greater numbers, they had to be tricked into allowing this to happen. The first thing the advanced humanoids (elites) did was to supply the "primitives" with a "god" to worship from among the ranks of the elites. This afforded the elites a large measure of control. They then instructed them to perform rituals that ended in the harnessing of the DNA coding and genetic material. Sound familiar yet? I know, right! There are some pretty eerie parallels between this and what took place in ancient Sumer! I guess T.V. and movies imitate reality a lil' more often than we would like to admit. So, could that be exactly why we were kept in the dark about so much? Are the elites of this world so

complicit with, and so eager to please their "needy deities" that they have orchestrated an elaborate coverup and manipulation protocol that has "miseducated" the masses of unsuspecting people,on this planet, for millennia!

Wow, I know that was a hard pill to swallow! It's easy and somewhat expected for one to feel angry that they've fooled us for so long. We must move past that and start to pathologically look at this process, so we can dissect, understand, and counteract this gastly plot! One of the worst things you can do to a people is to remove the knowledge of their true identity and origins, and replace that with utter falsehood! Then a "good slave master" teaches his/her new slave or slave race to trust only the information that is provided by the slave master. This is why the first move to completely indoctrinating and subjugating the new slave race, is supplying a "god" to worship that is in the image of the slave master! The religion establishes that a good worshiper is "god-fearing". Then the religion establishes that the slave masters are of the same lineage of the " god" to be feared and worshiped! The religion also establishes that a good believer has faith that the only truth comes from that religion and to question that demonstrates a lack of real faith! It may even demonstrate that the believer has been overtaken by darkness and sin if the questions persist! The topper is that the person's very immortal soul, is at stake! This is how billions on this planet have been so thoroughly controlled and manipulated by these elites. Think about it we uncovered earlier that between

Christianity and Islam there are over 4 billion followers! When one mulls over how coldly shrewd and efficient their methods are, it is not hard to see how they birthed shrewd economic concepts like capitalism! What other heartless systems have they taught us? What about the American language? That's right folks remember, it's not the same thing as the English language, as any good "Brit" will tell you. The American language, while derived from English mostly, is influenced by and contains words from many linguistic sources. That is likely why it is referred to a "bastard" language, by many. Anyone can learn this independently, with just a small amount of linguistic research. However, we have been guided to be very intellectually lazy when it comes to inquisitive thinking. Folks, when is the last time you saw a person pausing in the middle of one of their sentences to look up the entomology of a word, before continuing? We certainly were not taught to do that in school. We were just taught to memorize the content of the curriculum and conform to our scholastic requirements right? Also, we can't forget that as adults we are kept to busy, in the "rat race", to be distracted by something like inquisitive thought! I told you they were shrewd! So, let's recall little "Johnny" from chapter one. While his path of indoctrination was more direct, all of our children are educated in a way that does not threaten the paradigm established by this world's elites! Think about how effective their educational system is. The "fix is in" on our ever so bright children from pre-school students to college graduates to turn them to unquestioning, conforming, controllable kids. What about the term "kids". Have we ever

even questioned that label we blindly affix to our children voluntarily? Not only does the term kid refer to a baby goat, but with just a little research we uncover that in cult circles, this term also refers to youth sacrifices to infamous deities like "Baphomet". How inattentive, apathetic, and blind have we become that we do this to our children? The illogical loyalty to and usage of that term, by what seems like the whole of the good ole' USA , in my opinion, is only rivaled by the deplorable indoctrination of black people to fall in love with the word "Nigga"! However, that parallel seems fitting, given that the

"Racist White Supremacy Movement" was created to foster lasting separation, mistrust, and ill will between "Black" and "White" folks worldwide! This has only lead to the years of unspeakable and horrific treatment of indoctrinated (to be slaves) "Blacks" by the indoctrinated (to be the elites' slave handlers) "White" people. All this carefully crafted hatred serves the agenda of the elites perfectly! Is not "Divide and Conquer" the celebrated tactic of the methodical "war obsessed" mind? For a long time in this country, this separation was taught openly, in the school systems. It is vital that we understand this! I know people, I've been bombarding you with the problems that plague educational institutions. Yet, I do think that it is only by thoroughly grasping the depth of the root issues, that we can discover the best solutions to our worst problems (pathological thinking!).

Thus, it is apparent that, we need to rely on the method of tearing down flawed structures to replace them with solid structures. For our children we must substitute a flawed, distorted, and minimized education, with an enriching, open minded, civilized way of teaching that leaves our children far better suited to lead us all toward Peace, Love, Respect! Our children (not kids), are born with an incredible capacity to learn. We need to seize this opportunity with each and every child born! How do we do that? We must start with the first and most intimate teachers of our children, our wonderful women! Salute the mothers!!! We absolutely must treasure, honor, respect and appreciate our women to the highest degree! We must acknowledge and celebrate them, not just as mothers, but in whatever role they desire as they are more than capable! Tupac Shakur told us all about that! No more can we afford to allow our children to be taught anything other than to adore, honor, respect and look to our women for wisdom! Once we are successful at repairing the all important bond between our women and our children, we will begin to see progress right away! In order to do this we must recognize that the bond between Mother and child must not be interfered with during child birth! No more brainwashing our women into believing that the pain involved is so unbearable that they must submit to it by allowing incredibly toxic, psycho-active narcotics to poison their bodies and that of our children, during pregnancy & delivery! This hampers greatly the natural release of endorphins and cocktail of hormones, and other complex body chemistry that actually establishes the famed bond between mother and child. No wonder we sadly see so many coldly detached mothers with very little

connection to their child! Hey elders, this is why you find yourself shaking your head in disbelief at a young mother making her way down the street, seemingly inattentive to her children lagging almost a block behind. This distracted mother barely lifts her head away from that all important phone to check on the young children! This is not because, she is just a bad mother, or that young mothers aren't any good at mothering these days! It is often a result of the flood of (pharma-fixes) medications that American doctors just love to prescribe to these mothers before, during and after delivery! This must stop! It is terrible for the young child who never receives the raw nutrients that can only come from their mother's body! Not to mention the intense exchange of Unconditional Love and acceptance that happens during natural birth and breastfeeding! When a child has that they may now receive all the beautiful initial lessons that a warm, wise, and loving mother can and will share! This gives our children the needed foundation to receive a truly "proper education", one that benefits us all! Fortunately, there are some alternative learning centers that go along way toward teaching this way! For example, Hip Hop artist Wise Intelligent (formerly of Poor Righteous Teachers) largely supports the " Stevens Cooperative School, in Hoboken, NJ, with the proceeds from his cd's! We must promote, support and foster this type of "Free-thinking" educational institution! However, let's not just support that school, but open many great schools just like it! We have more than just a vested interest in our children, rather the ultra-high stakes of our collective future! So, again we undeniably need to emphasize this in our children's lives everyday, so that they grow up embracing how bright and unfathomably important they are! No more suppression of new ideas and inventions! No more being taught to just blindly produce and consume! No more allowing world governments and religions to stockpile the world's treasures of information and wonderful artifacts of the past, like the Vatican and all that is locked away and hidden there! No more elites sitting back and deciding what we need to know or not need to know! A perfect example of this is the way clean, renewable forms of energy have been suppressed, to keep the multi-trillion dollar fossil fuel industry alive! This is the education our beautiful children deserve and must have! Let's make sure they get it and change the world!

Chapter#7- "Environmental Responsibility"

When we think of our responsibility to our environment, what we are really saying is responsibility to our beautiful planet. We often, subconsciously, separate the two. It is our planet that has played host to us for our entire existence! It is our planet that has given all of us our material bodies, natural resources and the very atmosphere that we breathe and thrive under! It then seems rather foolish of us, that we somehow take all this for granted, as we continue to rape, pillage and poison our own planetary parent. It has been said that man is the only creature, that destroys its own nest! Well, we are all made from molecules and particles that are from this planet! We spring forth from her as dependent lifeforms, that cannot exist without our precious planet! This indeed makes her our planetary parent! Thus, one would conclude that it is virtual insanity that man poses the greatest threat to this planet that she has ever seen! What is wrong with us that we treat our only planet with such disregard? One may surmise that, we suffer a similar detachment from our planetary parent, as the detached child mentioned in chapter 6. However, we suffer this for a different reason. It is primarily due to the millennia of indoctrination inflected upon us, by the elites of this world! We have been programmed to have no regard for her. To do so makes you a silly tree hugger, in the eyes of most! Thus, we feel no responsibility for our reckless behavior toward our planet. We feel nothing, when we liter. We feel nothing, when we pollute. We have no guilt for not stopping these horrible "Fracking" companies from essentially digging into the body of this planet and cracking her tectonic plates to viciously pump poisons into her veins. Well, if our planets' crust is viewed the same way we view our own skin, we can better grasp these macabre attacks for what they are cold, calculating, and heartless methodology for savagely ripping our planet open to extract from her body whatever we want, for monetary gain! This is a sick mentality at work indeed! Yet, sadly it is our mentality, taught to us by these elites, who are sickly addicted to the gross amounts of money reaped from the fossil fuel industry! This is the same addiction to material gain that drives these savage minded individuals, who purposely keep this world in a constant state of conflict, simply to reap the "fruits of war"! Dosomething.org reports estimates that " Each year 1.2 trillion gallons of untreated sewage, storm water, and industrial waste are dumped into US water. While children make up 10% of the world's population, over 40% of the global burden of disease falls on them. More than 3 million children under age five die annually from environmental factors." Surfers against Sewage.org reports that every day approximately 8 million pieces of plastic pollution find their way into our oceans. There may now be around 5.25 trillion macro and microplastic pieces floating in the open ocean. Weighing up to 269,000 tonnes. Plastics consistently make up 60 to 90% of all marine debris studied". How much can our precious planetary parent take? We've got to be, like the worst children ever! I'm glad my children were nothing like that!

Pollution aside for a moment, what about the collateral damage of all the wars fought on our planet? How many mountains, grassy flatlands, deserts, oceans, rivers, lakes, and countless other bodies of water and land areas that have been seriously damaged (sometimes permanently), by our violent wars and other armed conflicts. Again, we seem to care not! We have seen broad and elaborate relief and rebuilding efforts carried out for cities and populated areas that have been devastated by senseless war! This of course is incredibly important. However, where are such efforts to aid and or rebuild those areas of our planet that have seen the destruction of man's wars over and over and over again!? Many have tried to holler out and make as much fuss as possible to come to our planets' aid. Yet, they are just easily pushed aside and dismissed. Sadly, it doesn't even seem to affect the elites of this world, or honestly most of us in general. To tell the truth, we are so indoctrinated that we have become completely distracted and consumed by the "rat race" of daily life! Again, this plays right into the hands of the elite, who only focus on the monetary profit margin! What about the alarming deforestation that has happened around the globe, particularly the surreal threat deforestation has meant to our wondrously picturesque rain forests!? Humans, under the direction of these elites, have endangered countless species of rare insects and animals within the rainforests, while absolutely destroying our rainforests almost completely!

I can continue to quote statistics, like about one-third of an average dump is made up of packaging material, that could have been recycled! I can state that the US population discards each year over 16,000,000,000 diapers, 1,600,000,000 pens, 2,000,000,000 razor blades, 220,000,000 car tires, and enough aluminum to rebuild the US commercial air fleet four times over. Both stats reported by University of Southern Indiana. Yet, we've seen the stats and heard the warnings from scientists and environmentalists. It seems to have no effect! Perhaps that is because our leaders have not backed them up! Just look at our current President (Donald Trump), whom has one of the worst mentalities and records on the environment ever! To make matters even worse, he seems to have a huge following in middle America (the Make America Great Again Gang), who totally believe that these problems don't even exist! They believe it's all political propaganda! I know this to be true! I've spoken with a lot of folks in these areas, with that mentality! As long as we continue to allow those persuasive commercials and guiltless button pushing politicians to determine this country's moral compass, we won't be able to lead the world into anything but peril! Thus, it's obvious that we must look to new leaders. We need to be sure that these new leaders have a good understanding of and a strong appreciation for our planet's worth. Far, too many

have already grossly undervalued our planet which has pointed us in the direction of an apathetic and indifferent mindset toward the one resource we ultimately cannot do without, our planet! This must be replaced with a mentality that truly demonstrates a mature, wise and cyclical approach to ensuring that we are always replenishing what we use from our planet, and adopting green technologies that protect, not harm her! If it appears that no such candidate exists, just remember our youth represent a pool of bright and intelligent future leaders that have the capacity to do much better! Especially, if we start to now teach them, early in life to value this one magnificent planet that we've been blessed with!

So let's leave them with some bread crumbs of what to adopt from our past generations that have shown a willingness to value Earth, and what to create to advance their efforts, and further establish a harmonious symbiosis between humans and our precious Earth! First, how and why have some groups demonstrated this healthy relationship? The Yoruba tribe of West Africa, The Olmecs of S. America, and the Native Americans are just a few who have had the proper appreciation for Terra(Earth). It is likely due to the perspective from which they viewed our planet, which was conducive to a cyclical lifestyle that aided them in this. They all shared not just a physical interpretation, but a spiritual way of viewing our Earth. They considered the planet a living, breathing entity (not just a big rock), to be respected and adored! Dare I say, they were right! Evidence of this bares out in the harmonious existence they enjoyed and the lack of damage to the planet. Thus, future generations must get back to adopting a similar perspective to ensure that they have a desire to do right by our planet! As for new eco-friendly technologies, we must stop under utilizing naturally occurring forms of energy ,all around us. It has been said in scientific circles that enough solar energy reaches our planet to more than run the technology of our current society. We are just so ignorant to this that we simply don't appear overly interested in this bountiful form of energy. Also one must consider wind energy, which is relied upon some, but nowhere near what we could potentially yield from it! Then of course, we should not forget about hydro-related forms of energy, on a planet comprised mostly of water, it just makes sense! These are just a few and that doesn't take into account the more exotic forms like "Zero Point" energy! We can and must carve out for ourselves a stable, harmonious, cyclically replenishing existence, on this one spectacular planet that we find ourselves perched on!

Chapter# 8- Agriculture

With certainty, one of the most important things we can secure for ourselves and our families is a healthy diet. Unfortunately, access to healthy all natural food products is somewhat scarce! Just take a walk through your favorite supermarket. As you stroll down the aisle, when you pick up an item that you may purchase, be sure to turn it around and carefully inspect the ingredients list. If you have grown accustomed to just picking up what looks good and tossing it in the cart, you may be shocked at what you find! Today's grocery stores are flooded with unnatural products with all sorts of artificial ingredients and actual toxins. In previous chapters, we've mentioned how our federal government has fallen way short of protecting us from the shady practices of agricultural corporations! It is these greedy corporate poison pushers, who are responsible for the lack of truly healthy, natural foods! As if the regulations set forth by our so-called protective agencies (like FDA) weren't loose enough, the companies even find creative ways to manipulate labels on the packaging. They can virtually state anything on the advertising labels, and state something almost completely different on the ingredients list! How many of you have picked up a food product that says " All Natural" and then turn it around to the ingredients list to see a list of artificial ingredients and toxins that are totally contrary to the advertising label that reads "All Natural"! The other day, I decided to check all the brands of bread in a local "Giant Eagle" supermarket. I must have picked up 20 loaves of bread before I found one brand that actually did not have a ton of toxins and artificial ingredients! Then of course, the one acceptable brand was also the most expensive brand of them all! Well there are two important factors here. One, is that we must take notice at the extensive effort taken to flood our grocery stores and supermarkets with food and drink that contains a myriad of unnecessary, unhealthy additives and toxins! The other nefarious thing to notice is the blatant intention to make the toxic foods much more affordable for lower income folks, even though they likely cost more to make with such a poisonous cocktail! They also make the healthy foods far more expensive to put them out of the price range for the lower income customers. It's an obvious targeting method! Then, because most of the target population is struggling to get by, we fall for this tactic every time we go to a store and purchase these poisons!

Many of these toxic additives are of some relation to calcium like calcium chloride or calcium carbonate. Simultaneously, there is the "chem-trail" program that we mentioned earlier, all of which falls onto our water supply, our crops, and the animals that most people eat! I talked briefly about how many soft metals and toxic chemicals have been found to be released in these "chem-trails", like these and other calcium related toxins!

Why? The answer is horrifying, yet simple! It's designed to spur on calcification of the pineal gland, along with poor health! Wait, let's think for a second about the investment being made here. First, the "chemtrail" program. This program has an incredibly broad range and scope, as planes emitting them fly across state and even national borders! On very sunny days they seem to run so many of them that the grid they create seems to near completely cover the sky! What costs are involved to pull off this monumental effort? What comes to my mind initially is the prohibitive cost of aviation fuel! Then, we must account for the cost of paying all those pilots! How about the cost of the actual materials being spewed from the planes? Wouldn't this also call for more time (man hours), for air traffic controllers, who must be allocated to keeping these additional flights, in flight paths that do not conflict with commercial, industrial, military, and private flights around the world!? What about all the border crossing mentioned, both state to state within the country and internationally? Think of the vast economic and political power needed for this! This is quite a pulling of world wide resources! It seems obvious that this could only be executed, by the "Hidden Hand"! Remember those shady guys? Now, let's turn our attention back to the toxic food program, and what is needed to pull that colossal endeavor off! Let's take a look at the scope of that program. We are talking about grocery stores, supermarkets, dollar stores, gas stations with food marts, school lunch programs, homeless programs, and low income food banks/pantries across this nation for sure and likely world wide! So, this involves an elaborate supply chain extending from production plants and warehouses to all of these venues. This would also call for thousands and thousands of business contracts and purchasing agreements. The logistics involved are staggering! All done with the underlying agenda kept secret! Yup, the "Hidden Hand" folks!

Now that we can adequately appreciate the extraordinarily broad reach of all of this, we need to look at the culprits executing this plan. We are talking about business owners, farming groups, store owners, fuel station owners, heads of intermodal delivery organizations, politicians in all three levels of government, advertising executives, and law enforcement! Oh, what an expansive an entangled web they weave! Unfortunately, hundreds of millions nationally, and billions internationally have been snared in this web of deceit, negative intentions and poisons! A major component of why this is so efficient and successful is the fact that the overwhelming majority of the targets of these covert attacks are totally unsuspecting! This is the reason for the intense secrecy surrounding this. The more behind the scenes these fiends can operate, the better for them! When you take both of these broad sweeping programs into consideration, you can see how truly immense the scope is! We cannot forget that there are government agencies (FDA & EPA at least) who've turned a blind eye to all of this! Again, this is a call for us to turn to new leaders! The ones in place now are not our representatives, at all! All the more reason for us to move expeditiously to replace them with individuals who are truly up to

the task, and who have our best interest, at heart! Currently, it may be difficult to locate such people. However, those numbers will continue to grow, as we make this information even more readily available.

This turns my attention to what is called "terminator seeds". The way this insidious invention works is that these seeds are almost forcibly sold to farmers to replace the seeds that the farmers crops normally yield. Then, when the crops grown with these new terminator seeds are ready for harvest, they yield no new seeds. In addition, somehow these terminator seeds make the farmer's soil inhospitable to normal seeds! Thus the farmers are forced to return to the manufacturer of these seeds for new seeds to plant more crops! What an efficiently deceptive plan! Hmm, I wonder who is responsible for the production of those seeds? Instead, let's think again about motive. For such an unbelievably large and broad scoping scheme, there must be an equally as important motivation for these elites to go through so much trouble! What are they looking to accomplish? Better yet, what are they desperately trying to prevent? Recall that much of this is aimed at the intentional calcification of the pineal glands of billions of people! Wow, there is obviously something about the prospect of all these folks walking around with decalcified pineal glands that scares the daylights out of this world's elite! This tells me that the a world of "awakened" masses is perceived as a threat! This evidently explains why there is also a simultaneously implemented and intricate effort to drastically shorten the lifespan of said masses! That is why they go through such great lengths to bombard us with toxins and poisons from so many unsuspected sources! One has only to visit the "Georgia Guidestones" and read carefully to see the vision of this world's elites. They envision a massive population reduction from approximately 7.5 billion humans on Terra to only 500 million, a much more controllable new slave population! Will we get back to planting our own vegetation, controlling our crops, and protecting the purity of our foods, water, and air? They are counting on our apathy, confusion, and our attention being distracted from the constant "rat race" and indoctrination! Will we just sit back and watch this happen? Again folks don't take my words for a warning or truth, find it yourself! To quote the famous T.V. series " The X Files"........" the truth is out there!" When you find it, pass it on!

Chapter#9- Healthcare VS. Holistic Wellness

Have you noticed in recent years that, when you visit an emergency room you seem to often leave with no answer as to what's actually wrong with you, just a prescription? I and many folks I know have experienced this first hand. I have found myself wondering, "how and why am I being prescribed drugs when these doctors don't know what' wrong with me"? Honestly, It's a rather perplexing question that I faced quite frequently and gives me pause. How can I have trust in these medical professionals, when they seem far more interested in pushing pills and giving injections than pathologically finding my ailment? The answer is, truthfully I don't trust them. I can't trust them, when it appears obvious that my well being is 2nd to maintaining their predetermined agenda. Then, to take a closer look at this, I can clearly see the agenda in place! It's, once again, a demonstration the the huge "out of control" Pharmaceutical Industry works hand in hand with the American Medical Association, to keep a constant flow of medications (drugs) being prescribed to U.S. citizens. This doesn't even take into account O.T.C. (over The Counter) pharmaceuticals. In 2015, the U.S. spent $325 billion on retail prescription drugs (drugs purchased at pharmacies and through the mail, as opposed to those administered directly by doctors), according to the Centers for Medicare & Medicaid Services. Last year, nearly 4 billion prescriptions were filled in retail U.S. pharmacies. (1) California filled about 300 million prescriptions alone. When you combine the two in your mind it isn't difficult to realize that Americans are way over medicated! Berkers Hospital Review.com reports the 10 most popular prescription drugs for 2017 were the following:

- Vicodin, Norco, Xodol (hydrocodone, acetaminophen) Drug class: Opioid/acetaminophen combinations. ...
- Synthroid, Levoxyl, Unithroid (levothyroxine) Drug class: Thyroxines. ...
- Delasone, Sterapred (prednisone) ...
- Amoxil (amoxicillin) ...

- Neurontin (gabapentin) ...
- Prinivil, Zestril (lisinopril) ...
- Lipitor (atorvastatin) ...
- Glucophage (metformin)

Is there any wonder, as to why there is an opioid epidemic? Yet, that problem has been building for years, in this country! This build up coincides with the increasing trend of over prescribing many medications, to patients who may or may not have had a medical necessity. Talbott campus.comreports, in the US alone, an estimated 54 million people over the age of 12 have used prescription drugs for non medical reasons in their lifetime. Most abused prescription drugs fall under four categories, based on the number of people who misuse the drug:

- Painkillers – 3.3 million users
- Tranquilizers – 2 million users
- Stimulants – 1.7 million users
- Sedatives – 0.5 million user

These figures don't even take into account the multitude of medications (some experimental) that are commonly forced on psych ward patients! I mentioned briefly how throughout history many individuals have been persecuted, ridiculed, imprisoned, and or confined in mental institution. Unfortunately, it has been an ugly aspect of human behavior to take such blind reactionary steps, when confronted with an individual(s) whom may have opinions that are so radical or unpopular that society proves unable to accept them! Despite this tendency having been uncovered long ago, society still leans toward these tendencies! It is very disappointing, if not sad to think that in 2018 someone could lose their freedom and be confined to a mental hospital just because someone else says that they are crazy! Sadly, the accusers are often family members, with an ulterior motive! How many sane people, who may just be stressed or have some other copeable issue, are locked away in a mental facility that is only concerned with keeping those who are employed there supplied with a job, and needlessly pushing medications on patients, who don't really need all those drugs? That doesn't even bring to question all the side effects, that these folks suffer through, while ingesting these toxic narcotics! The Rosenhan experiment or Thud experiment was an experiment conducted to determine the validity of psychiatric diagnosis. ... The study was conducted by psychologist David Rosenhan, a Stanford University professor, and published by the journal Science in 1973 under the title "On being sane in insane places". This study backs up the horrifying idea that there are folks whom could be productive members of society, but instead are confined to these mental institutions for long durations (sometimes life). These folks unable to defend themselves forced to swallow, or forcibly injected with heavy psycho active drugs that have the ability to reduce a normal person to the state of a virtual mental vegetable! They are often repeatedly misdiagnosed by "mental health professionals" just to keep the beds filled! Many of these psych doctors are not very qualified. However, some of the worst culprits are very well qualified, as again the A.M.A and The American Psychiatric Nurses Association (APNA), and other officially recognized mental health associations turns out far to many glorified habitual pill pushers! This is a very scary aspect of our nations attitude toward mental health, which is an extension of how this country approaches

healthcare, in general! More people report using controlled prescription drugs than cocaine, heroin and methamphetamine combined. That puts prescription drugs second behind marijuana when it comes to illicit drug use. Realistically, that makes prescription drugs #1, as most people these days wouldn't consider marijuana an illicit drug, the increasing popularity of legalization efforts reflects that. Remember folks, it takes a doctor or otherwise legally permitted health professional to have written all these prescriptions! Even EMT's seem to have changed drastically over the past 25 years or so. I can offer this as a personal observation having taken 4-5 ambulance trips over that time span, not to mention a multitude of stories relayed to me by family members, close friends, and associates. We all seem to agree on this.

I do not convey these facts, in efforts to demean or discredit the thousands of dedicated and caring medical professionals nationwide! We need and truly appreciate their advancements in saving lives and all of their help, but these concerns are far too serious to not be raised! Now, with this knowledge we need to be turning our focus toward solutions and alternatives. What has worked? Who has been effective in healing people? What are some of the more successful types of medical treatment? What preventative measures have yielded the most success? To attempt to find sufficient answers to these pertinent questions, I shift my attention to Holistic Wellness.

Holistic medicine is typically broken into 5 categories. These categories include: Acupuncture, Ayurveda, Homeopathy, Naturopathy, and Asian medicine. Holistic medicine is an overall philosophy that considers the whole body of a person, including the body, physically, psychologically, socially, even spiritually ... Holistic doctors use various forms of health care such as conventional medicine with a focus on promoting natural healing. The American Holistic Health Association (AHHA) describes it this way: "Rather than focusing on illness or specific parts of the body, this ancient approach to health considers the whole person and how he or she interacts with his or her environment. It emphasizes the connection of mind, body, and spirit. In many healthcare circles outside the influence of western medicine, spirituality is absolutely key to implementation of Holistic Wellness! In fact, many holistic practitioners tend to include multiple holistic disciplines in their treatment regiments. "Whatever is best for the patient" is the more frequently found mindset of these practitioners. Which is a welcomed far cry, from the unfortunate tendency to focus on pushing expensive and often detrimental drugs to patients, all to commonly found in "western medicine".

Another truly significant aspect of Holistic Wellness is adherence to an all natural "plant based diet". This is essentially the patient's best natural effort to keep the body in a healthy state of readiness to fend off disease and ailments. Well what of more physical damage related issues, like a broken bones? There are methods of dealing with that as well. Many such methods may seem as strange as they are unconventional, an example would be "healing a broken bone with a certain type of wet mud"! The very

basic idea of holistic medicine is not to introduce foreign stimulants into the body, to promote healing. Rather, to stimulate the body naturally and internally to arrive at the desired healthy state of being! Our bodies are essentially capable of healing just about any illness or ailment with only natural assistance and internal prompting. We often underestimate the incredible design of the human body! Also, we tend to disregard the fact that the human brain is the command center of the body! When our brain is operating at full capacity and with clarity of purpose we are capable of healing in some incredible ways just by meditation and concentrated thought! I can attest to this personally! I'll share an inspiring story. Some years back, I became rather good friends with a co-worker of mine, Ms. Char. She and I worked together and shared many details of our personal lives. After having worked together for a while, I noticed that she was developing a lump or growth on her neck. She confided in me that the lump was cancerous tumor! Later that year, she explained that even after enduring several forms of chemotherapy, her doctors had given her 6 months to live. The same dreaded death sentence given to my deceased Father, many years prior! This saddened me greatly, but not miss Char! She said" don't worry about me honey, they aren't the authority over me. I ain't going nowhere!". " My Lord is the ultimate authority!". Then Ms. Char began to change everything about her lifestyle that did not serve her well being! She adopted a very healthy diet, high in fruits and vegetables, and avoided anything artificial. She essentially adopted the previously mentioned all natural plant based diet! I only worked there with Ms. Char for a few months more. She and I eventually fell a bit out of touch. When I finally bumped into Ms. Char again, a couple years had passed. She was as healthy and happy as I ever had seen her. The cancerous lump on her throat was gone! I didn't have to inquire how, she just looked at me, then pointed to the sky and smiled! I understood quite well, and her story inspires me to this day! I have also been made aware of some very interesting theories of how powerful the human ability to heal is, from within the meta-physical community! It has been stated that the human spirit has the power to control the materialization of the body! This essentially points to school of thought that we incarnate our physical form from thought form, using concentrated thought and intense concentration! Recall that we've already proven that everything is constantly in motion, referred to as vibration frequency. Therefore, one could consider materialization, as a form of motion. Also, given that our bodies are a collection or gathering of atoms, wouldn't the pulling together of those atoms to form a body constitute motion? Perhaps, the science of this isn't quite as fanciful, as it may first seem! This actually touches some on the concept of re-incarnation commonly embraced by many schools of thought. It is suggested that we are capable of de materializing and then re materializing in your original DNA dictated physical form minus the ailment or injury! Remember, that DNA has scientifically proven to be one of the most efficient means of storing and passing along information codes and data. Its capacity is

absolutely incredible! No matter whether you are open minded enough to contemplate that or not, there's no doubt how incredible our bodies are and that "if we take care of our bodies, our bodies will take care of us! So let's never be, as lazy thinking, as many view "Western Medicine" to be! Let's treat our bodies right and heal!

Chapter#10-

"A Just World Economy"

There are two very important factors in our present world financial systems that are in serious question. Those two factors are the U.S. Dollar and the economic philosophy of Capitalism on a whole. Let's attempt to deal with the first of the two, the Dollar. The U.S. Official Inflation Data, Alioth Finance, 20 Dec. 2018, https://www.officialdata.org/1980-dollars-in-2016 reports that " The dollar experienced an average inflation rate of 3.01% per year during this period. In other words, $100 in 1980 is equivalent in purchasing power to $291.27 in 2016, a difference of $191.27 over 36 years. The 1980 inflation rate was 13.50%." This demonstrates a significant difference in the inflation appreciation that the U.S. dollar enjoyed during the turn of the decades between 1979 and 1980. Raw data for these calculations comes from the Bureau of Labor Statistics' Consumer Price Index(CPI), established in 1913. According to this data Americans felt the greatest rate of inflation in the areas of Medical Care Services 5.39 % increase and Medical Care Commodities 4.49% increase. Here, we see yet another indication that medical expenses have grown considerably as a burden for citizens.

In Nov. of 2018, www.thebalance.com reported that the value of the dollar today is much less than it was in the past. When the dollar loses value, it's called inflation. That's when prices rise, so your dollar buys less than it used to..... The dollar's strength increased 28 percent, but by 2018 it had fallen 14 percent. A weaker dollar buys less in foreign goods. This increases the price of imports, contributing to inflation..... This boosts the United States' economic growth, which attracts foreign investors to U.S. stocks. But, if enough investors leave the dollar for other currencies, it could cause a dollar collapse. There are guys in suits, who get paid a lot to have these debates, and make such predictions. That is not our focus. It merely serves as the back drop, for the real work in thought we must all do, in considering where we're headed!

One thing for certain is that, we have been given a fairly murky outlook for the future of the U.S. dollar. This is backed up by fiscal information, from many different sources. Simultaneously, we are generally seeing a world shift toward digital currency. Perhaps, this shouldn't come as a huge surprise given that just about every aspect of our "modern" lives has become digitized! Even human beings are having micro chips inserted into them. That's right folks, there are currently parents who are electing to have their own children implanted with "tracking chips", so they wouldn't be kidnapped or lost. This has been done for years, with pets. Also, we do now live in a society, where customizing our children before birth, has truly become a reality! Digitization has indeed permeated our society. Can it really be unexpected that we would soon be operating in a paperless society, with only digital currency? Doesn't a simultaneously collapsing U.S. Dollar add to the possibility of, not only digital currency, but a world with one digital currency that is accepted internationally? Doesn't a world with only one digital currency seem just a step away from a world with only one governing body? Is that the beginning of the "New World Order", so frequently speculated about?

The other factor is the popularity or lack there of for the system of capitalism. If we were to take an approval pole, much like we do with the U.S. Presidency, we would see that capitalism has a rapidly decreasing approval rating. Perhaps, this can be attributed to impact of the "information age". Americans, while still heavily indoctrinated, are having much more debate over the fairness and lack of equality found where capitalism lives! They are seeing rather frequently, these days, the effects of a mentality of " hey let's freely capitalize off of the misfortune, economic hardship, starvation, pain, and misery of the rest of the world to our benefit"! It doesn't sit right with many of them, as it shouldn't! Less and less people are falling for the old U.S. company line that we're just "spreading democracy and freedom"! They are wising up to the sobering facts! We (the U.S. and its citizens) are the usurpers of the world! You may say, "wait not me"! However, every time an American has a material need or want that is fulfilled within our capitalistic economic system, we are benefiting from the hardship of someone else on the planet! The is simply how the system is designed! We have allowed this monster to grow to the point that nearly our every purchase is made "on the backs of" and "at the expense of" what we call the "third world". This term, in itself, is a degree of separation that we have adopted to be able to psychologically accept our self centered and abusive reliance on capitalism! There is a great little 20 minute video that I saw on YouTube called "The Story of Stuff"! The video was presented by the Tides Foundation, Funders Workgroup for Sustainable Production and Consumption, and Free Range Studios. This video accurately and intricately depicts our dependency on finite systems that do nothing to replenish the resources, that they so rapidly deplete! The video also shines a bright spotlight, on the true reality of Capitalism and how it is implemented by the world's elite! We have literally tricked ourselves, or rather allowed ourselves to be easily tricked into thinking that the rest of the world is just "jealous of our freedoms"! No They are justifiably angry at our greedy systems that use them and their resources to appease our selfish demands and wants! Once again another hard pill to swallow folks, but GULP! This is the real world, without those blinders of indoctrination and complacency, that we've grown so used to! A former co-worker of mine, used to always say "Oh well! not my house!". This was his typical way of saying, it doesn't matter to me what happens to anyone else, anywhere else, "as long as I got mines"! As a nation, we have become this numb to the struggle and suffering of others, all for the sake of getting

what we want! Again, it's not entirely our fault. Not when every time you expose yourself to any form of multi media you are also being exposed to the very indoctrination that drives us to feel so indifferent and consumed in wants rather than needs! Don't we teach our children about the difference between what they need and what they want? Or do we? Perhaps, we have forgotten that all together. Certainly, we need to admit to ourselves that we must mature as a society, and be willing to admit responsibility for our world wide impact, and how much our economic ideology broadens feeds that very negative impact! Here, we find ourselves with another Michael Jackson "Man in the Mirror" moment!

So, with that in mind, what work needs to be done to establish a "Just World Economy"? We've already uncovered that the first area of growth along these lines is in our mentalities. We can no longer afford to view others as the burden bearers of our wastefully sustained lifestyles. There is no such thing as the third world!!! We cannot perceive ourselves as better or more deserving than any of our brothers and sisters across the world! Location doesn't determine human rights, humanity does! Remember the truth people, we are one! Once we can adopt that basic philosophy, and begin to teach the next generation that mentality, it only makes sense that we will do much better, as they become the new leaders taking office! Once again, our children are truly our future! However, we must wake up to find truth, in order to teach it to them. We must be brave and wise enough to take the blinders off! We also need to be mature and alert enough to know that they are there, in the first place! It will call for us to escape our confines of apathy. There are a lot of things that keep us in that place! Those of us, whom suffer from alcoholism and chemical dependency, may struggle a little more. Those of us, who have found wealth will find it much harder to see the inequality and lack of fairness, that our current way of life highlights! It is already, and will become even more difficult to to look past our circle, to the needs of folks with less. Yet, we need to do it! Perhaps, it would be more doable, if we learn to no longer embrace that which has made us so cold and indifferent, to the well being of others! It's our ego that must go! At least, the ego can no longer run the show! We absolutely must mature past the "me,me,me" mentality that our egos have so fervently toiled to place at the forefront of our thinking! Why has this been so deeply rooted in our psyche? It is primarily because we have fully and wholeheartedly entrenched ourselves in this toxic influence. We must self evaluate and train ourselves to identify every instance of selfish motive. That will be particularly hard for most, as we are not in the habit of even thinking about our actions at all, let alone examining our true motives with any clarity! Our society has been guided to constantly seek solutions, to what ails us. Even though, for the most part, there's nothing wrong with us! It is simply the illusion of lacking that we are suffering from! Right here in the United States, if we adopt unity consciousness, we could end domestic homelessness and hunger tomorrow! This can be accomplished just with completely

even distribution and redistribution of all of our resources! You don't need an economist or some other suited professional to see this people! Just readjust your thought pattern, to not think with ego! How many millionaires do we have in this country? How many billionaires? How large of a house do you really need, to provide shelter for your family? For some of us, how many houses do you need? Do you just have enough clothes to have 3 changes of clothes, or do you have closets full, so you can be stylish? How much food does it take to provide a person with enough food for sustenance? How much food do we throw away everyday? Now with all that in mind, think back to that person you just walked by (sleeping on the sidewalk), while you stroll leisurely down the street, or splashed by in your car? I know folks, it's not so much fun to look in the mirror! I feel you, really I do! It takes a lot to mature to this viewpoint! It often comes from going through some pain, particularly the pain of loss! Sadly people, it often takes for us to be knocked off of our high horse, and to lose all that which we hold dear to see clear! Like many of us I have felt that loss! Rather than leave me broken, it broke me down and enabled me to be rebuild from a new foundation! A much stronger foundation! Dare I say that, we must collectively rebuild our foundations to support a new, more mature mentality! We must also soften our cold, hardened hearts, to be empathetic toward others! When we truly feel the pain of others, in our hearts, we will be driven to end all the needless suffering! It is only with this new way of thinking, and feeling that we can turn the corner to developing a new truly equitable "World Economy"! However, I warn that we will only accomplish this, if we take on the great task of drastically changing how we teach our young folks, and holding those currently in power, to a new standard of fairness and equality! We can do it! So there, it remains for us to do!

Chapter #11 -
"New approach to Technology"

We have indeed learned quite a bit, on this journey we've embarked on together. Nearly everything we previously accepted about life has been challenged, right? Have you been thinking, as much as reading? After all, it's not my truth that you are responsible for finding! It's your own! Hopefully, you have had several instances when you've had to drop this book and do a little research to challenge what you've read. If not, you've certainly left yourself a little bit of work, right?

So, let's continue down the rabbit hole and out the other side refreshed with some answers to all these questions! Now, I think we should change our focus toward finding new more green technologies. To do this, we most likely need a new approach. This seems necessary since, our current approach to technology has lead us to these finite systems that only steer us toward depletion of our resources, rather than replenishing what is used! We need cyclical systems that are designed to both satisfy our needs and replenish what has been used, and or systems that work interdependently to replenish each other. The perfect example of the direction we need to look in, is the relationship between man and plants/trees. We actually help each other breathe! In fact our symbiotic relationship is nearly infallible as humans breathe in oxygen (rather we extract oxygen from air), and breathe out CO_2. While, plants breathe in CO_2 and expel the oxygen that we need to breathe! This is exactly the way we need to be interacting with our planet. Folks, it's not just a coincidence (nothing really is) that humans and plants benefit from each other in this way. This planet is incredibly rich with resources, many of which we have yet to discover! Perhaps there are some that we need to re discover. At any rate, it is completely feasible that humans conceive and develop holistic, cyclical systems that work with our beautiful planet rather than continue to rely on systems that only deplete and destroy! There are already some bright and hopeful forms of energy creation and harnessing of clean energy that go hand in hand with an agenda of nurturing and protecting TERRA! She deserves that at the very least from us! Some of these green forms of energy include "Hydro" power, "Aero" (wind) power, and "Solar" power! However, it may be more pertinent to address the more troublesome forms of energy that have already yielded adverse environmental issues. Given historically recent events, we can look no further than nuclear energy technologies. Right now as I type, there is a continuing meltdown of a nuclear reactor plant in Fukushima, Japan. That doesn't account for the reactors that had to disastrously go off-line in Chernobyl Ukraine, USSR and the Three Mile Island

accident in Pennsylvania, United States! Being a resident of Pittsburgh PA, how can I forget that one? I do not mention these to suggest that nuclear energy is not a viable form of energy, only to state that we need to learn more before we can guarantee clean usage! I would be negligent to not mention the harmful electrical technologies that plague us today! Wait! Huh? Are you trying to tell us that we shouldn't even use electricity now? No, I am however, disclosing that a lot of today's electrical tech is harmful. Most of today's electrical technology emits what is known as E.L.F. waves! What are E.L.F. waves? Extra Low Frequency waves! Extremely low frequency (ELF) is the ITU designation for electromagnetic radiation (radio waves) with frequencies from 3 to 30 Hz, and corresponding wavelengths of 100,000 to 10,000 kilometers, respectively. In atmospheric science, an alternative definition is usually given, from 3 Hz to 3 kHz. We are also adversely affected by GWEN towers. The Ground Wave Emergency Network was a command and control communications system intended for use by the United States government to facilitate military communications before, during and after a nuclear war. They are both forms of tech that are very harmful to the human nervous system and harmful in other ways, including psychologically!

What I most believe, needs to be refined is the approach, we take conceptually when we create new technologies or move to improve current tech. Human beings have always displayed brilliant flashes of creativity. It seems to be when our minds are the most free and at ease that we create best. Throughout our time on this wonderful planet we have shown that we can work with what we have. The incredible ability of human beings to adapt is remarkable! We have oft faced long odds, just in our survival. This proves to some degree that it's actually survival of the" most able to adapt" rather than survival of "the fittest". Our adaptability is the one trait that has separated us, from other species that have not fared as well, on this planet. Fortunately for us, this trait lends itself to discovery and advancement. Whereas, we adapt as we learn what works best. This sets us up to create, learn what's better, and then adapt to adopt the better tendency. This is commonly known in the business world as improving by adopting and sharing "best practices". In this way businesses can constantly improve! Human beings do the same process to continually get better. We do, however, need to correct our mental approach to creating and inventing, by having a truly open mind and not just accepting new ideas, but encouraging them! We cannot afford to turn down or turn away any ideas from any person or source. Listen folks, we have an entire world to reshape! The only way we'll accomplish this, difficult to imagine task, is to embrace all, as contributors to the process. We definitely cannot slide back into the old paradigm, where we shut down certain people, and label them as crazy! We cannot shut down certain ideas and dismiss them as impossible! We cannot look at the monumental nature of the task in front of us, as one that is too big for us to handle! I covered earlier how the revolutionary ideas of Nichola Tesla have been suppressed for decades! I have

also mentioned how the fossil fuel industry has stood as a constant blocking mechanism, preventing us from enjoying clean, renewable sources of energy, and green technologies in general! Greed! Selfish, self eroding, implosive greed has lead us to the brink of destruction. In fact we're essentially teetering on the edge of the abyss! All because of myopic greed, we have allowed these more than helpful ideas of clean technologies to be kept hidden by those who benefit mightily from the toxic, finite, broken fossil fuel industry! We must only allow those in decision making positions, whom exercise the good judgement to never see such stagnation and oppressive limits of access to valuable ideas! If these tremendously useful ideas and technologies are to be beneficial, we must mandate an atmosphere where the development of such creative thinking is fostered openly!

Inventors throughout history have been met with skepticism socially, to say the least! Sadly we've treated such persons more like enemies than valued friends. Is man's psyche really so fragile that the mere prospect of something that would bring change frightens us to exhibit rash, reactionary behavior! It is a curious aspect to man's development, that we have such stances toward the very people who introduce lifesaving, innovative, important ideas, theories, and experiments to us all. Change is the only thing in existence that is real and constant! So, wouldn't it be far more logical for us to embrace change? Wouldn't it demonstrate far more adaptability for human beings to seek to thrive under change? After all, let's not lose sight of the fact that the goal is to always be able to adapt! This planet is constantly changing, and now appears to be in a period of great change! Scientists generally agree that the center of our galaxy is spewing out enormous, uncharted energy dispersals! This is in turn affecting the stars in the galaxy to do the same in each solar system, in this galaxy! Our Sun is no exception to this phenomena. The sun is spewing out incredible energy dispersals of many forms, which has a very profound effect, on our planet and its inhabitants! That means profound change for us! Therefore, it is likely that now more than ever we must approach the prospect of forming new technologies with open clear minds, and accepting change. Practically, I propose that the talented young minds that are being shipped off to MIT or some prominent Ivy league destination, be enlightened as to how important they are, in this dawning of a new age! I would love to see them embrace their important roles and keep their talents and valuable minds home to aid in the discovery of new technologies that benefits the world, rather than corporate America and the world's elite! We, as the parents, grand parents, aunts, uncles and friends of these special minds need to support them fully, in that effort! We can't be petty! We must really totally support them, in every way. It's not a free ride we're providing. We will all benefit in the long run from their intellectual efforts! Let's literally provide for them, as we recognize that the studying and work that they do is vital to us all! Just as we need healthcare for all, we need to educate and foster the growth of our special young minds

to be all they can be. It's time to not just say the "children are the future", let's invest in them, rather than Wallstreet! Again, we must also hold our representatives and decision makers accountable to us, for a change. We must have legislation that brings this to fruition by relaxing or eliminating school loan debt! We need better green education that emphasizes how beautiful and valuable our planet is ,and why what they create should work in harmony with her! We've seen enough ways to harm and usurp her! We need to not only see a renewed valuing of the student, but also re education of the teachers to adopt a free thinking, truth seeking and speaking curriculum that grooms our youth to be free thinkers and unshackled producers of the kinds of new revolutionary technology we need! Our classrooms should explode gleefully with creative energy, and spontaneous excitement for learning! Though, I have focused on the new technologies that our children can create, anyone can and should contribute! I even have some ideas myself. I would like to see us develop mastery of magnetic energy! In particular, I would like to develop mastery of null fields. They are energetic fields of resonance between positive and negative poles. Oh well, just a little something I was thinking of! Perhaps, you have pondered some form of tech, yet to be explored! I have no doubt that if we are all working to develop our creative ideas around technology, surely we'll be amazed at the results!

Chapter #12 -
"Open Minds"

Mentality. There have been many reasons given throughout this book to prompt us all, to change or grow our mentality. I have stated several times, in several ways, that we need to deal with all of this with Open Minds. However, I find myself asking what is a truly Open Mind, and how does that refer to how we must handle all of this subject matter? Well, certainly the opposite of open is closed. Logically, if one wants to understand how to exhibit an Open Mind, they would display characteristics that are opposite of a closed mind, right? It seems to make sense to me, so I'll run with it! A closed mind is generally convinced, that whatever knowledge they have is all the knowledge there is to know. They would also tend to assume that whatever conclusions they've drawn are correct. A closed mind generally doesn't lend itself to debate, or even discussion, for that matter! A closed mind doesn't readily accept new concepts or ideas, no matter the source. A closed mind is just that, generally closed to input! I think we can see pretty clearly, why we could not effectively address any of these issues, with a closed mind. How can one adopt new ideas, methods, and concepts when their mentality won't even allow the introduction of such material? Because of this, an Open Mind has a natural enemy, the ego. Remember, the ego is purely selfish! It wouldn't actually accept anyone else's thoughts or opinions, because such outside stimuli are irrelevant. Effective problem solvers are typically not closed minded, or egotistical. They are generally humble and open minded. You know, Wise! We most definitely need to be wise to tackle this host of substantial problems. Of course, there is also the fact that, pathological problem solving totally lends itself to the discovery of new solutions, facts or implications of newly uncovered knowledge. We could be very philosophical in our attempt to understand what we mean by an Open Mind. However, for the purpose of problem solving, and mining solutions we'll concentrate on more practical applications of an Open Mind. For example, to read this book(especially unsolicited) requires a person to have an Open Mind. The individuals who tend to spend hours viewing informative videos on Youtube and reading informative books, has an open mind. The other trait they are exhibiting is the previously mentioned thirst for knowledge! Some folks, just naturally have that. Some others may not, yet have a strong enough curiosity that they are willing to entertain different schools of thought en route to finding their truth! Again truth is in the mind of the seeker of knowledge, much like how beauty is in the eye of the beholder!

In proceeding chapters, we have encountered many obstacles (natural and man made) that obstruct our path to truth! We have learned of layers of indoctrination, public ridicule, institutional safeguards that guide us away from learning and steer us toward simply believing without questioning. All of these factors and more combine to limit, the openness of our investigative process. Remember those pesky elites, who just hate when you think pathologically and with an open mind! Many such obstructions have been purposely put in place! It seems to be the highest priority to those elites to essentially keep you in the dark (in terms of information), while they stay "illuminated" to the facts of our situation on this planet! We have uncovered a great many problems and found a great many avenues to find solutions and answers! This is not what they want! You play right into the hands of said elites, when you are closed minded, and cut off from openly communicating with one another! So, Simply don't be that way! Why give back all the progress we've made here and with other "freedom in print" efforts? Why go back to the ignorant bliss of just not knowing and not asking any questions to find out any answers! We must proclaim in a unified voice "No More!" "We won't go back!" Then just move forward! We can only do that with a mind that is free and inquisitive! We can do it with a mind that is truly opened! It is when we make our oppressors upset that we can know we are on the right track. We have no excuse for not researching, in this information age, when all you seek to learn is at your fingertips, literally. All we need is to be critical of all information and not be too lazy to fact check.

"Do the knowledge people"! It's past due for us to get back to using common sense, "trust your gut"! Remember, if it doesn't make it past your B.S. detector, that's probably because it's B.S.! Don't be swooned by any suave and charismatic presenters, with their eyes on the prize, your mind! Be just as impressed with yourself for taking this journey as you are with those presenting information. You are just as impressive, in your own way! You are just as capable of digesting this information, at your own speed! Each of us is a different, yet equal part of the greater solution! We can do it together if we value each other and each other's opinion equally! It is only the drive of ego that wants to always be right and someone else always wrong! When the truth is that we are all just different pieces of the puzzle! Thus, we can never allow anyone else to close our minds. We cannot allow resistance or fear of change to close your mind! Don't allow complacency to close your mind! Stay with an Open Mind and let's discover our truth together!

We also need to do a better job of searching out new things to be learned about our planet! The more you know about a person or thing, the more you are attached to that person or thing. How can we be of a mindset to protect our planet, if we don't know about our planet enough to feel some attachment? I have sprinkled in a few things about this planet, throughout this book. For example, the ancient name of our planet referenced by many civilizations. That name is Terra! This is where the term

terrestrial or extra-terrestrial comes from. I also mentioned briefly, how there are habitable subterranean ares of the planet. Did you know that there are theories about entire civilizations that live in similar subterranean parts of the planet? Did know that theorized area of the planet has been named "Agartha"? Did you know that there is only one man in history, who has lead major expeditions to both the North and South poles? That man is Admiral James Byrd. This man has revealed in several interviews, that he has some evidence of some truth in the theories about subterranean Earth. Some of the things he reveals in those interviews is very surprising to say the least! However, I'm going to leave you with the work of actually reading the interviews for yourself! Then, of course, there are all sorts of theories floating around about the shape of the planet. You have the new "Flat Earth" people. Then there's the ever popular "Dome" theory. These two represent the kind of theorizing that I see, as not the best use of my time. However, they may present a path to your truth. I find a few things about "Agartha" to be rather interesting possibilities! Such as the possible existence of something called "heavy water". "Heavy water" is hypothesized to be not just water with just a slightly more dense molecular structure, like ice, but actually $H3O$. Notice the extra hydrogen molecule, if compared to typical $H2O$. I must admit, my childhood excitement, around this "near discovery", given my affinity toward the old "G.I. Joe" cartoon that featured a segment where they searched for "heavy water"! Just the possibility is very intriguing to me! Also as a Western PA resident, I can attest to there being some fairly sizeable caverns that are available for public exploration. Some archeologist and other scientific specialists suggest that literal county sized caverns may exist! This, as well, proves to be rather interesting to many exploration minded folks. Yes, the earth's land mass still holds many mysteries, yet to be solved! However, ponder for a moment that we (human beings), have yet to explore the majority of the Earth's bodies of water. That represents a great deal of exploration yet to be done, since most of the planet is covered by water! The possibilities for discovery are virtually endless! We may, eventually, find out so many new things about our very special planet! We may encounter many new species of life! We may uncover new plentiful natural resources! We stand to learn so much, with intense research and expeditions into this remaining frontier!

Speaking of which, how could we ever forget, "the Final Frontier"? Star Trek fans (Trekkies) would flip! We have an unfathomable amount of discovery ahead of us when we think of space, "the Final Frontier". My eyes gleam with excitement about the opportunities for discovery, that come with space exploration! I can only imagine the incredible beauty of being able to eyewitness a colorful nebula, or to witness the birth of a new star! The potential wonders and unbelievable sights, that one would undoubtedly encounter on such an exploratory voyage, are overwhelming! I would have to sign up! Perhaps, I will at some point in my life! Even boring old conservative Ronald Regan spoke about space exploration and the possibility of contacting, or being contacted by

new civilizations. Our current U.S. President actually spoke about the U.S. developing a "Space Force" as a new branch of the military. Hopefully, not all those in high ranking federal positions will approach space exploration as a military priority. I think it is vital that, we enter deep space exploration with a peaceful and scientific mindset! Remember PEACE, LOVE, RESPECT! I would say that this approach to life is just as important "off planet" as "on planet"!

In all of our Open Minded accounting of exploration possibilities, we should be sure to include further exploration of what we call "inner space". There are many scientist who would exclaim that "inner space" is likely just as vast as "outer space", and perhaps not all that different! Whatever the focus of our exploratory pursuits, we must proceed forward, with clear compassionate hearts, childlike zeal, and our most Open Minds! Surely the potential and inclination toward discovery showcases some of man's best qualities to share with all!

Chapter #13 -
"We are One"

This is a fun chapter, for me folks! I am an enthusiast, when it comes to unity! Since I was a young boy, I've maintained some vision of unity, in a peaceful world. Although, at different stages of my life, my behavior did not always reflect that. That's right, even Mr. PEACE, LOVE, RESPECT, has had periods of not being peaceful at all, in fact, I was quite violent. I actually got into a lot of fights, early in life, for many different reasons. Now, that I have grown and matured, I see those reasons, largely as excuses. They were excuses to not do the hard work, frequently associated with "keeping the peace". Fortunately, I've grown out of the immature mindsets and tendencies that made obtaining peace difficult for me. However, it certainly didn't happen overnight. It was a long and challenging process, to say the least. It was a struggle! I gained and lost a lot along the way. I'm sure that many of the mistakes, that I've made in this process, have made life much harder for me, than it had to be. Although, now that I can appreciate the entire process, I understand that it had to be that way! Everything about my journey contributes to the man I am now! In fact, I now feel that for each person, the process to mature and grow is a major reason why we live our lives and experience separation on many levels. I also believe that each of us has a mission, to find how we can contribute to the growth and maturation of the collective, on a whole! We are all contributors! Yet, that doesn't exactly explain my acceptance of the concept of "We are One". Perhaps for that explanation it would be better for me to begin somewhat scientifically. It has been proven that neither matter nor energy can be destroyed, only altered in state. Undoubtedly, humans are comprised of matter and energy. We touched on these concepts, earlier in this book. In fact, it is accurate to state that all things are made of energy on some level! All of the known universe is comprised of energy, in some form or another. Speaking in pathological terms, when we retroactively think of the universal creation we are left short, if we adopt the "big bang" theory. We are always left with questions like "where did those first particles of matter come from? What was the catalyst to spark the big bang? Where did the immense energy needed to create the universe come from? Also, how can we just completely ignore all the signs that point to intelligent design? We are left with the unavoidable conclusion that some vast and unfathomably intelligent energy source always must have existed, and always will exist! Now, for many folks (like me) that constitutes a higher power. Which to me, is another means of which to express, our CREATOR's magnitude. Which is also an exercise in futility! Truthfully, we simply don't know! Even though, that seems to be the last thing that many of us wants to admit. However, logic suggests (que the Mr. Spock reference), that since all energy still exists once it has existed, then whatever is in existence now, has always existed in some form, and always will exist in some form. Therefore, it is in fact that all things energetic (all things), must spring from the same energetic beginning or source, and end in that same energetic source! It only makes sense! We cannot escape the reality that, "We are One"!

Earlier, I quoted the famous R&B group Frankie Beverly and Maze, and their song "We are One". The lead singer has a line where he talks about the "silly, silly games we play, when we try to make each other feel so bad!", or something like that. This is reflective of current human behavior, on this planet. It tells of our interaction both on a planetary scale and on a scale as small as the microcosm of the family unit. We have become so immersed in this illusion of separation, that we are constantly acting toward the next person, in a way that is not indicative of how we would want to be treated! It is exactly the opposite, of what we need here. We sincerely need to commit ourselves to treating others how we want to be treated! This is to say that we will no longer uphold the pervasive mentality of separation, that we have subconsciously adopted. Most people today, have a difficult time grasping that we are energetic beings living in physical bodies. Therefore, it is that much more difficult for them to comprehend, that all are at least somewhat, connected on an energetic level. I have detailed in this book many ways that the separation mentality leads us to ruin! We just cannot afford to let it hold us back any longer! To do so, would only feed the destructive objective of the elites. Anyone who desires to live in PEACE, LOVE, RESPECT will not align themselves with the agenda of the elites! It's time for change! That change must be physical, spiritual and mental, for each individual. It is only in this way, that we can collectively grow together. This growth will foster and spawn more unity consciousness and less separation illusion. Thus the inhabitants of this stupendous planet, we have been blessed with, will mature to align with the hermetic flow of the universe! It is only at that point that we can become the higher beings that we were always intended to be! I was just over a friends house, and he introduced me to his younger sister for the first time. After some time, it occurred to us that although we were all different ages (45,26, & 22) that we had no problem enjoying fun, intelligent , and stimulating conversation. We had such a good time talking freely about multiple subjects, without any obstacles of age, race, religion, sex or background differences holding us back, that we lost track of time! Time raced by so quickly (as it does when having fun), that I had to leave abruptly to honor another engagement! However, what I walked away with from that quick little fun time, was the limitless, boundary dropped exchange that we shared! Wait for it! It's as though we were connected! With plenty of differences before us, it was somehow easy to find a comfortable common ground. If we search for it with Open Minds and warm hearts, that common ground exists for all of us! We can reach it and find the same calming Peace! Next, we will feel our beautiful, collective Love! Soon, we will have Respect for all of our CREATOR's creations! It is only then that We can and will truly be One!

Chapter #14

Moving Forward

Forward. Always Forward! The words of "Pops" come to mind again. As I reflect a bit, the way I tend to do. I am reminded that I must always focus my gaze forward. Forward is the direction of change, and change is the only constant. Thus, the prepared mind is best equipped to adapt to change. I had to get "all logical" on y'all right quick"! Come on, we can laugh a lil' together, right? It's apparent to me that we won't be able to keep our morale up through all of this, unless we can laugh a lil' or a lot! We must maintain our sense of humor through all of this pain that we have to process and let go of to Move Forward! Rebuilding isn't about our hearts breaking, at a tearful ending, it's about embracing and celebrating a new beginning!

The slate is clean now! The Earth or Terra or Great Gaya and all inhabitants can breathe a collective sigh of relief! It was long and hard! It was an arduous task, but we had to get through it together. That's what we've done! I say that with the confidence of someone who knows the outcome. Well, there's a reason for that, I do know! If anything, I've always credited myself for being a man of vision! Anyone with any real vision has the knack of noticing trends, many consider it a scientific discipline. It doesn't really require much vision to take note, what I've witnessed, recently! I've noticed people returning my smile with an even brighter smile as I greet them in the a.m. I hear more and more folks deeply satisfied and gleeful at my standard reply when anyone asks "how I'm doing", Excellent! I know western P.A. may be a fairly small sample size, but trust me we were loaded with "grumpies"! Also, recently spent some time in Baltimore, MD and Chicago, IL, where I experienced the same thing! I'm often doing work that puts me in communication with people from all parts of the country, sometimes the world! It's what some would call uncanny. I can almost feel it in the air. I almost borrowed from the great Phil Collins song with " the air of night"! Really though, It's almost tangible that, while the few extremists dominate the news headlines, the general mindset of the "average person" is opening up to change in so many new ways! The closed mentality is finally dying out, and compassionate open hearts are shining through the murky clouds of separation mentality to the brilliant promise of unity consciousness! Don't get me wrong folks, there's a ton of work ahead of us, yet to even begin! However, I remind you that we just have to notice the "beginning of a movement" to see the cresting of the wave! I assure you, that's just what's coming! A wave of consciousness that will be as beautiful, as it will be transformative! You can see the quiet rumblings of it in the eyes of the people, anxious with hope! If you look for it! It will

only be evident in the eyes of a person who approaches the beginning of each day with hope! I and many others have grown even further to adopt anticipation of the good outcome. To expect the "happily ever after". Anyone else remember when, even if you felt lame a lil' you cheered on the underdog! Even, the little guy gets to win, sometime! There are some who, are anticipating an actual energetic wave to eventually overtake the planet, when its Schumann Resonance (vibration frequency) reaches 5th dimensional resonance! There is some science to that given the recent energetic solar emissions, mentioned earlier, in conjunction with the recorded spikes and new plateaus of the Schumann Resonance. When you factor in, some of the other pieces of evidence that we've uncovered, the scientific basis for the argument is there. However, that is not my focus. I merely need to be another kindling on the violet fire that must burn away all the evil, ill-intent and negativity that has so insidiously permeated our collective psyche, via the control of the elites! So, yes upon further reflection regarding this book, I feel confident I've done that! After all, that just means my job is to make you think a little or a lot! It's those thoughts that are the ripples, of a wave of change, that I feel humbly honored to take part in!

Allow me to offer up my best rendition of the "Ivy League" close. In summation, it is henceforth concluded that the collective awareness of man/mankind is not only susceptible to, but has in fact been influenced negatively in the past by low frequencies and positively in this present by higher frequencies! In other words, we had been sucked into a dark world when we look at it honestly and with clarity! Yet now, we are poised to embark on a massive positive shift in consciousness or awareness, for all those willing to work on self! Introspection is one of the best, yet least oft used tool in our spiritual tool belt. It can give us the necessary insight to make much needed changes physically and mentally as well. Some have termed this the "self accusing spirit". Whatever phrase or term you are more comfortable with, the point is we have the tools to get the job done, with willingness to work! I hope that in some way I may have helped someone, in writing this book! Even, if it's just that you are "rooting for the underdog" by reading this book. I hope that this has been a pleasantly surprising journey, that you've taken with me! One in which, we've grown together! I thank you all, with all my heart, for reading this and just for being you. For, I appreciate and love you all, as the bright energetic beings you are, who shine warmly through the smiles that I hope to see multiply with PEACE, LOVE, RESPECT!

Acknowledgements:

My undying love and gratitude for a lifetime of love and support to the following: My Mother-Darlene My Father- Charles (deceased)

My Step Father- Michael (deceased)

My Co Parent & Lifetime friend- Regina

My Son-Daniel

My Daughter- Aisha

My Son-Osei

My Sister-Terra

My Brother-Levar

My Brother-Michael jr.

My Nieces & Nephews

My Uncles & Aunts

My Cousins-Currys, Andersons, etc...

My Extended Family- The Vaughns Family

My Close Friends

My Acquaintances

Dear deceased loved ones- Sisters, Grandparents, Aunts,

Uncles, Cousins, Nieces, Nephew, Close Friends, Acquaintances,

My Hometown- The City of Pittsburgh, PA……..

With this I hope to inspire thought, open hearts and minds, and spark a movement of positive change for this world of ours! Thank you all eternally!

Made in the USA
Monee, IL
07 November 2021